DYEING WOOL

Karen Schellinger

Schiffer Publishing Ltd

4880 Lower Valley Road, Atglen, Pennsylvania 19310

DEDICATION

This book is dedicated to Frankie Carlotta Bushey, my very best friend, teacher, and mother. Mom showed me what compassion is, what it means to share, and how to help those in need. She was an entrepreneur and she spoke to everyone, leaving them with a smile on their face. She was a giver. She knew about this book project before ALS (Lou Gehrig's Disease) took her away on her birthday, October 26, 2008. I miss her.

"With the Angels," designed and hooked by Karen Schellinger, in memory of Frankie Carlotta Bushey, mother and friend.

Other Schiffer Books on Related Subjects:

Color and Fiber. Patricia Lambert, Barbara Staepelaere and Mary G. Fry, 0-88740-065-5, $49.50

The Creative Hooker. Jessie A. Turbayne. 978-0-7643-2645-5, $39.95

Copyright © 2010 by Karen Schellinger
Library of Congress Control Number: 2010924174

Designed by Stephanie Daugherty
Type set in Hazel LET/Zurich BT/Gil Sans MT

ISBN: 978-0-7643-3432-0
Printed in China

Schiffer Books are available at special discounts for bulk purchases for sales promotions or premiums. Special editions, including personalized covers, corporate imprints, and excerpts can be created in large quantities for special needs. For more information contact the publisher:

Published by Schiffer Publishing Ltd.
4880 Lower Valley Road
Atglen, PA 19310
Phone: (610) 593-1777; Fax: (610) 593-2002
E-mail: Info@schifferbooks.com

For the largest selection of fine reference books on this and related subjects, please visit our web site at:

www.schifferbooks.com

We are always looking for people to write books on new and related subjects. If you have an idea for a book please contact us at the above address.

This book may be purchased from the publisher. Include $5.00 for shipping. Please try your bookstore first. You may write for a free catalog.

In Europe, Schiffer books are distributed by
Bushwood Books
6 Marksbury Ave.
Kew Gardens
Surrey TW9 4JF England
Phone: 44 (0) 20 8392 8585; Fax: 44 (0) 20 8392 9876
E-mail: info@bushwoodbooks.co.uk
Website: www.bushwoodbooks.co.uk

CONTENTS

ACKNOWLEDGMENTS

A very loving thank you to my husband, Leo, for his patience while I used our limited and very special time together to complete this project. He is my grounding force, my friend, and my reason for being. He appreciates and respects my creativity, and my need to share my knowledge with others. His support does not go unnoticed. I will love him always.

I believe it takes many fibers to make a cloth. The unique cloth that I am at this moment is the result of the many fibers of "teachers" and numerous examples of sharing which I have experienced. I needed them all.

I send a special thank you to Stephanie Ashworth Krauss, Director of Green Mountain Rug School. Due to a chance meeting with Stephanie, a kindred spirit who loves wool, I have taught dye classes in Vermont for the past seven years. The dye class has been a great success and has developed into several levels: essential, comprehensive, and advanced. Grown from mutual respect and a love of fiber arts and color, our journey has evolved into a very special friendship.

Thank you Jessie Turbayne. I have collected all of Jesse's books, published by Schiffer Publishing, and have attended her lectures. I will always be grateful to have her as a friend and guide in this world of book making.

I feel strongly about giving credit to other women who have craved color and dyed wool. These women needed to hear their own color voice then somehow apply it to their craft. My teachers have included Marion Ham, Patsy Becker, Marianne Lincoln and, of course, Jane King. If there was a color or dye class available, I signed up for it. Of course there were fees attached, but as Elsbeth Kramer, my friend and former student taught me, there is no value in free.

A sincere thanks to: Marion Ham, Mary Williamson, Nancy Elliot, Patsy Becker, Jane King, Margaret Howell, Sherri Heiber Day, Dianne Stoffel, Marianne Lincoln, Jessie Turbayne, Marjorie Judson, Heather Ritchie, and Pat Chancy.

I mentioned Patsy Becker earlier; I just know her dye pans are cooking in heaven. A perfect example of kindness with pizzazz, Patsy's teaching skills were beyond amazing; she did it all very well. Watching her blend color in the dye pans was a privilege I will never forget. Patsy introduced me to Pro® Wash Fast Acid Dyes, and that was my blessing. A very big thanks, Patsy.

Thanks to Tina Skinner who was on site when I visited to Schiffer Publishing to take the photographs for this book. Encouragement is very important for a novice in the world of book making, and Tina calmed all my fears. Thank you for keeping me on task.

Special thanks to the Doug Congdon-Martin and the photographers at Schiffer Publishing. While on my visit, their professionalism and high standards were obvious. The camera and lights were set up for me and, with a little instruction, I was able to take the photographs in this book. I learned a great deal, and my confidence grew with positive feedback from Doug.

All the wools dyed in this book were donated by Terry Dorr of The Dorr Mill Store. Unless noted all of the textured wools in this book were donated by Pat Cross, Charlottesville, Virginia.

Kind acknowledgements to Chris Kane, Chris Rabeneck, Karen Handmaker Zina Howe, Vicki Jensen, Pat Cross, Adale and Terry Woodruff, Heather Trautman Bourroughs, Ivana Vavakova, Harley Bonham, Ken Haines, Terry Dorr, Doug Grey, Linda Spear, Bonnie Roycewicz, Gaye Guyton, Nancy Jewett, Linda Reinhart, Karyn Lord, Celeste Duffy, Sue Getchell, Kathy Knisely, Jackie Gauker, Laura Dillard, Linda Beaulieu, Elaine Fitch, Glenn Cotton, Robin Garcia, Peggy Corr, Phyllis DeFelice, Larry Bushey, Leo Schellinger, Malinda Tuttle, Mary Beth McClure, Martha Rosenfield, Barb Buren, Karen Beatty, Pam Passafiume, Sara Fredrics, Sue Raymond, and all of the others who contributed to making this book, directly or indirectly.

Most of all, thanks to all of my amazing dye students over the years, I would not be teaching were it not for their desire to learn more about color and dye techniques. My first students in Charleston, South Carolina, brought paint chips for me to reproduce in the dye pans for their particular blue. I can never thank you enough for those early challenges.

Now to the many students that traveled to Vermont to take my class, thank you from the bottom of my heart. You put your trust in my skills to transfer what I do in the dye pans into usable tools you take away. All of the students bring with them a cup to be filled with knowledge that will make a difference in their fiber art. I also learn and grow with the students in the classes. I watch the students amaze themselves as dye color meets wool and they realize they have created gorgeous dyed fabrics in the dye pans. It is pure joy.

During my travel to Vermont, I have formed friendships with as much intensity as the color in my wool. There is not much time to visit while there; however, one memory stands out for me and it would not be fair to our fiber journey if I failed share this story. I had the opportunity while teaching in Vermont to have JoAnn Millen in class. A fiber artist in her own right with varied interests, she had taken several Shibori classes. I had been teaching only the essential level dye class, until one year when Joanne handed me a Shibori-dyed piece of wool. That was the beginning of the advance dye techniques class. I took that one piece of wool and designed a class around it. Other advanced techniques expanded from the basic techniques aided by my culinary skills. Joanne, thank you for sharing your talents and life lessons with me, so that I may grow in life and learning.

FOREWORD

oday's fiber artists offer compositions that are aesthetically pleasing and monetarily valuable to an ever increasing and appreciative audience. Discriminating artists are selective when it comes to the use of color. Fiber enthusiasts are no different. Historically the challenge faced by all artists is how to achieve those "perfect" shades, tints, and hues.

A mentoring fine arts professor once told me, "Artists are people who view the world with great intensity." Karen Schellinger is such an artist. Possessing a contagious zeal for life, she sees color and creates color with great intensity.

This, her much anticipated first book, draws upon a dye master's vast experience, and expertise. Allow Karen to guide you through her world of color. You will enjoy the journey.

—Jessie A. Turbayne

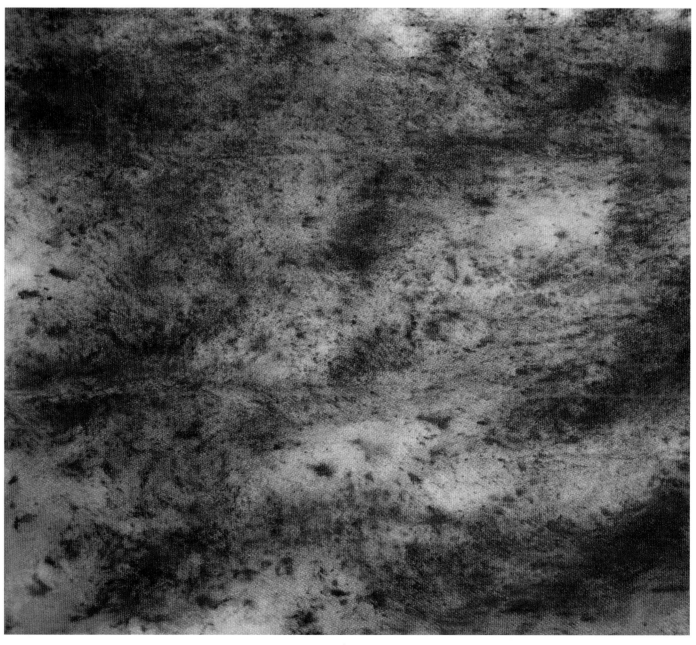

Dry Dye Technique

INTRODUCTION

Welcome to Karen's Wool Garden, where color grows wild. Wool is my fiber of choice when making traditional hand-hooked rugs, quilts, and penny rugs. The techniques and dyes presented in this book may be used on any protein fiber. If other fabrics such as cotton or silks are used, consideration is given to the correct dye to fabric relationship recommended by PRO Chemical & Dye Inc®.

I consider this project a dream come true and a blessing. It is a privilege to have the opportunity to pass along the wisdom of color and fabric manipulation in the dye pans through these dye techniques. This book takes you on that journey using dye lessons, fabric manipulation, and color relationships.

Many of my former students are weavers, knitters, spinners, and quilters. They have brought their wool fibers to the dye class in different stages. This book is not limited to fabric in its finished form. Several techniques have proven successful with roving, yarn, and slightly felted wools.

This book is a result of teaching essential and advanced dye classes using Pro® Wash Fast Acid Dyes on wool fabric, at Green Mountain Rug School in Randolph, Vermont; Stephanie Ashworth Krauss is the director. This workshop is one of the oldest

Graduates of the Advanced Dye Class, 2007, in Randolph, Vermont. L to R: Gaye Guyton, Linda Spear, Karen Schellinger, Bonnie Roycewicz, and Nancy Jewett.

Dyed wool hangs to dry during the class at Green Mountain Rug School, in Randolph, Vermont. It is always fun it is to see the flags of color chosen by the students.

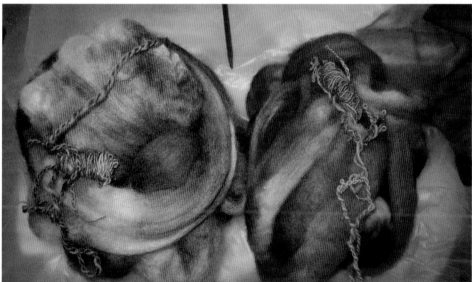

Linda Reinhart brought her undyed yarn to the 2009 dye class on red day. Linda and the rest of the class dyed fantastic reds starting a very colorful wool stash. The yarn was processed the same as wool.
Courtesy of Linda Reinhart

Roving was brought to the Vermont dye class and proved to be a fun challenge. We dyed our chosen colors while maintaining contrast in color and intensity. The roving was processed the same as wool fabric.
Courtesy of Judy English

traditional rug hooking workshops in the USA. In June of each year I may be found in Vermont, and the other months teaching in my home studio in Louisville, Kentucky.

Many of these techniques have been passed down to me like great family recipes. I have incorporated my culinary skills into the techniques to manipulate the wool and, then, add dye in whatever creative ways possible. For example, the Shibori techniques, an old Japanese tradition, involve creatively folding, wrapping, and/or stitching silks prior to adding dyes. I have modified those amazing techniques to wool.

While I continue to push the wool/dye relationship as far as possible, I follow the manufacturer's recommendations from PRO Chemical & Dye Inc.® for each of their products.

I am constantly wowed and still very excited by the colors and dye placement coming out of the dye pans. My hope is that this technique book takes you on a journey of color, experimentation, and, mostly, fun in the dye pans while building

"Star Flowers." Design and background wool is by Karyn Lord. Another fun way to use dyed wool, the top colors came from my collection. This is my first attempt at making a penny rug.

confidence and independence. My own personal goal for you is to learn to "dye by eye" without formulas; however, examples will be provided with a formula in each chapter.

I was always busy taking notes in former dye classes, afraid to miss important information. Later, I found I could not read the notes...too much scribble... and that, with my head in the writing, I had missed the concept of the technique. Hindsight has taught me I should have been watching instead of writing. We all learn differently, so I have provided pictures and words to appeal to all learning styles.

Many women come to the class in Vermont with excitement, trepidation, and an eagerness to learn. By the end of class, students have experienced the color and dye technique relationships. They have mastered the techniques for making secondary and tertiary colors by eye, recognizing that it takes practice and know-how.

A close up, showcases the added dimension in the orange flower and green stem. This is a result of color choice and dye technique. Appliqué is my personal favorite when quilting wool or cotton. Pattern is by Karyn Lord.

Patsy Becker blew me away in one North Carolina workshop. She sat me down at the table with blue, yellow, and red dye dissolved in separate cups, and in 5 minutes taught me how to make a color wheel on a paper towel. At that moment I knew I could learn how to create color without fear and wrap my head around this world of color and dyed wool. I followed her around in the dye kitchen for a week and, because of her sharing, here I am.

If you have no dye experience, I recommend that you start at the beginning of this book as though you were attending a workshop. If you are experienced, skip to a technique that you may have not used before. Use this book as a resource and a color journey meeting your personal needs to enhance your fiber art. It's great fun. Never worry, there are no mistakes, only more dyed wool. Surround yourself with the colors you enjoy.

—Karen Schellinger, M.Ed., 2009

Right: "Groovie Graffiti," designed and hooked by Chris Rabeneck. Chris uses dyed wool from the techniques in this book for traditional rug hooking. *Courtesy of Chris Rabeneck, Louisville, Kentucky.*

Life is full of color in different textures, intensities, and values. Utilizing the techniques in this book, create a well balanced stash of dyed wool ready to be used when you are.

COLOR SENSE

Every day we rise from our beds and dress ourselves. In dressing, we may not realize it, but we have made a color selection, a choice by which the colors in the garments appeal to us, make us feel good, or complement other garments. It is that simple. Every one has color sense, but we may not be aware of it or have had enough experience in how to use it.

One year a very comical student continuously asked for muted colors, like autumn leaves. In class I helped her to meet her requested goal of a "muted gold," but as piece after piece of wool came from her dye pan, she never smiled at her results. I loved the golds, so I couldn't understand why she seemed so disappointed. I finally asked her to look at the mounds of dyed wool around the class room and show me a color or two that made her heart sing. She walked right over to jewel tones, very intense bright colors. I informed her she favored a jewel tone palette, not a muted or pastel palette, and she smiled for the duration of the workshop.

Take a walk around your home and notice the colors present there. Note how the colors make you feel in your individual rooms. Is it more comfortable in the living room than the kitchen? Does the bedroom feel warmer or cooler than the living room? Is there one color item that jumps out at you when you are in a particular room? We respond to color both visually and emotionally; color leaves an impression on us and others.

I had a client come to my home for business. As she was leaving, she said, "You know your home is very comfortable to me. It's very warm. If your colors were cool and in blues, I would not have come back." Color impacts us strongly and every individual may be passionate about different colors. This is a good thing.

One very wise teacher (I will not give her name away) amazes her students. She disappears into a room where her wool is stashed and brings out the exact color that happens to be your favorite. It goes right into your rug, the perfect piece, and you love it. How does this very experienced teacher help you color plan your rug in your favorite colors? I will share the secret. During the workshop, her wardrobe remains almost neutral and she is very aware of the colors you wear to class. How could you not love what she brought to you, if you have been wearing some value of it daily?

Colors evoke emotion and, in working with our fiber arts, it is very important to have a working knowledge of how color relationships work together.

Nature surrounds us with color and we may borrow any color we like. Depending on your geographic location and the season, all around us is a color garden. While the cold seasons may present a more neutral palette, whatever the season, we have a virtual classroom of color every time we experience the outdoors. It is a fantastic and free training tool at our disposal.

Your color sensibility is always expanding and changing. From this first chapter, I want you to take away the awareness of color that surrounds you daily. Just like your speaking voice, you have a color voice. I want to help you find it.

NOTHING TO FEAR

By being aware of the colors that surround you and knowing which colors make you happy, it becomes easier to experiment with colors and to mix them. Color theory plays an important role in understanding color. I find there are many books that talk about color and are most helpful. I have listed my favorites in the bibliography.

In my own color journey, it was as if Patsy Becker had said to me, "You have permission to learn about

An assortment of colors and textures. Wool rolled this way demonstrates how it looks when used in traditional hooked rug. This wool stash is the result of a 2-day private dye workshop at my studio, Karen's Wool Garden in Louisville, Kentucky. Wool dyed by former student Ivana Vavakova. *Courtesy of Ivana Vavakova, New York, New York*

color." Then, I realized it was less important to need permission than it was to know I could learn about color, and then find teachers willing to share what they knew. It is a "learning," as one of my favorite people, Julie Marie Smith, said one day. I want to learn every day and, if I am open to it, a lesson is available.

The art stores are full of books with amazing artists describing how to mix blue, red, and yellow together to create paint colors. As fiber artists, we borrow the color concepts and theories, and then apply the knowledge to mixing the Pro® Washfast Acid Dye colors into our dye bath. You do not have to be born with artistic abilities. As you learn more about color theory and apply the knowledge in your medium of choice, color blending will become second nature to you.

Start now. Begin by identifying the color of an object before its other attributes. Does the grass appear yellow green or blue green? Does the flower have a red purple or blue purple petal? It takes practice to see the color first, but it will be such a great tool for you to use.

RED, YELLOW AND BLUE

It will be essential to learn the basics of color theory prior to mixing the dye colors for a smoother journey in the dye pans. I find this to be the first step toward mixing a dye bath with confidence. Memorize the primary colors and what combinations make the secondary colors. These are the keys necessary to unlock the world of blending colors.

Primary Colors are colors not made from other colors:

Blue—Yellow—Red

Secondary Colors are colors made from combining 2 of the Primary colors together.

Blue + Red = Purple
Red + Yellow = Orange
Yellow + Blue = Green

HUE...The Name

Primary + Primary = Secondary

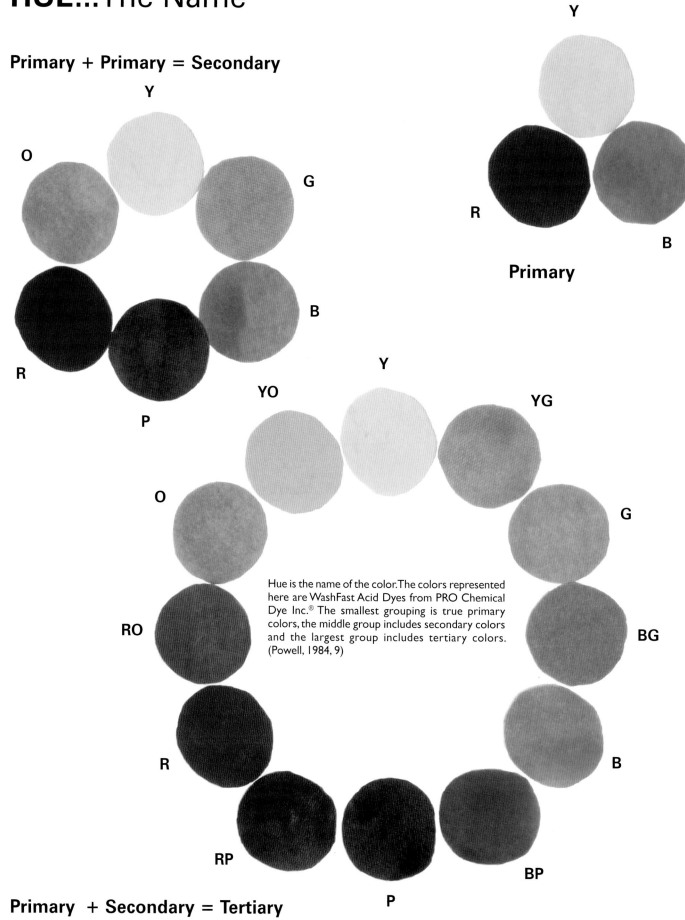

Primary

Hue is the name of the color. The colors represented here are WashFast Acid Dyes from PRO Chemical Dye Inc.® The smallest grouping is true primary colors, the middle group includes secondary colors and the largest group includes tertiary colors. (Powell, 1984, 9)

Primary + Secondary = Tertiary

VALUE...The Most Important Quality

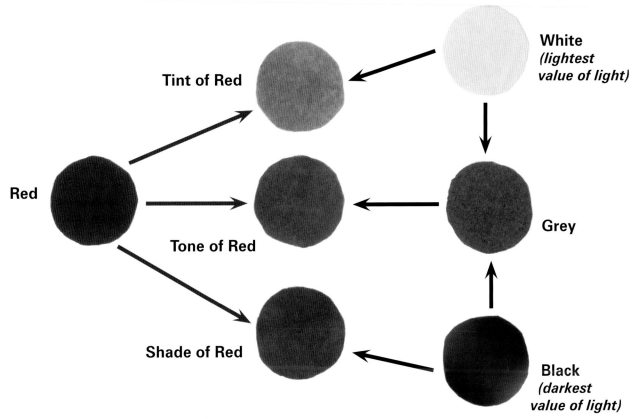

The Lightness or Darkness of a Color

The value of a hue is influenced by the addition of white, black or grey. A color may lighten or darken, but will remain the same hue. When dyeing wool we may begin with white wool or a very weak dye solution for a tint of a hue. *(Powell, 1984, 14)*

INTENSITY...Purity or Strength of a Color

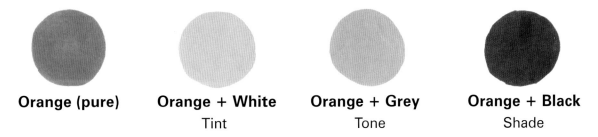

Orange (pure)	Orange + White	Orange + Grey	Orange + Black
	Tint	Tone	Shade

The intensity of a color shows the strength or purity of a color. We may alter the intensity of a hue by adding black, brown or another color. A weak or strong dye bath also changes the intensity of a color. *(Powell, 1984, 23)*

Color Wheel

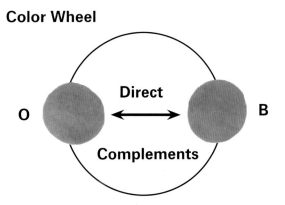

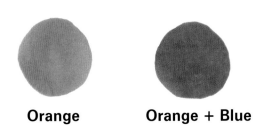

13

"Where's Noah?" designed and hooked by Pat Cross, Charlottesville, Virginia. The relative relationship of light, bright, dark and dull are well balanced in Pat's favorite colors and intensity. *Courtesy of Pat Cross.*

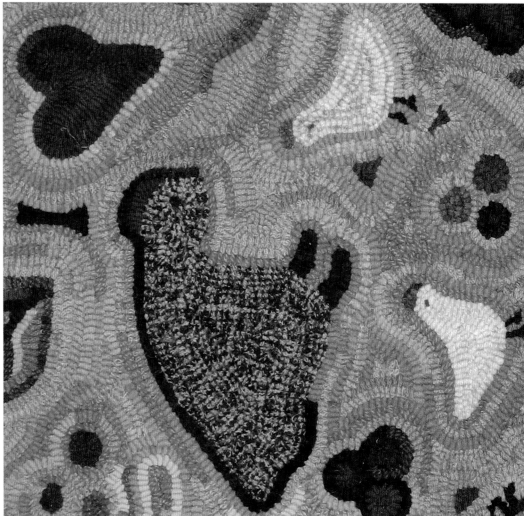

A detail of Pat's rug shows the variegated neutral background and the level of color intensity. *Courtesy of Pat Cross.*

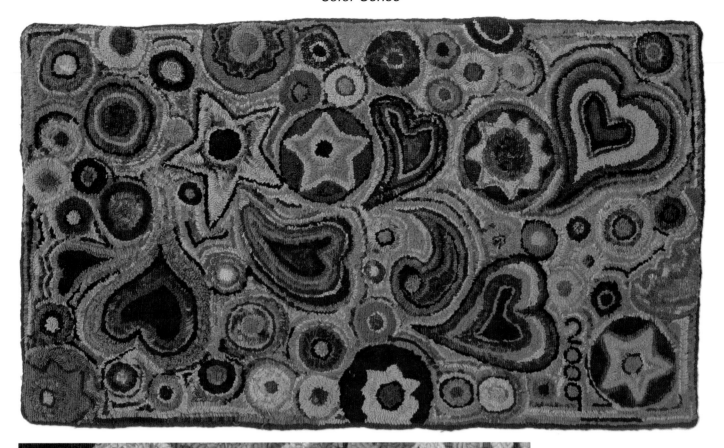

"Groovie Graffiti," designed and hooked by Chris Rabeneck, Louisville, Kentucky. The relative relationship of light, bright, dark and dull are well balanced in Chris's favorite colors and intensity. *Courtesy of Chris Rabeneck.*

A detail of Chris's rug also shows the variegated neutral background and the level of color intensity. Note the similarity of rug's design and background choice, but different color intensity, yet both pleasing to the eye. *Courtesy of Chris Rabeneck.*

To summarize, all colors are made from the three primary colors: blue, yellow, and red. By mixing two primary colors together, you will create a secondary color, purple, orange or green.

ORANGE, GREEN, PURPLE

Since the secondary colors orange, purple or green are made by combining two primary colors together, by definition one primary color is unused. The unused primary becomes the direct complement of the secondary color created. All direct complements are directly across from each other on the color wheel.

As an example, I make orange from combining red and yellow. Blue is the unused primary color. Looking at the color wheel, we find blue directly across from orange. They are direct complements to each other. Now, if I combine some amount of orange and blue I would find my dye bath to hold some value of grey or brown, because combining a color with its direct complement will always cause this result.

The same holds true for purple, a combination blue and red. The primary yellow is unused, and yellow is directly across from purple on the color wheel. Varied amounts of the direct complements will result in some value of grey or brown.

Combining blue and yellow primary colors together results in green. The unused primary color is red, which is directly across from green on the color wheel, and becomes a direct complement relationship. Combining these direct complements in some varied amount will lead to value of grey or brown.

To summarize, **Direct Complements** are colors directly opposite each other on the color wheel. These colors grey or dull each other when mixed together in different amounts. They also make great values of brown:

Blue + Orange = Brown
Yellow + Purple = Brown
Red + Green = Brown

If you know the color basics before you start mixing the dyes together, you will fly through the lessons this book has to offer. When I teach my dye classes I purposely have a "blue day," followed by a "red day," and then a "yellow day." The dye bath starts with the color of the day. The primary color days are followed by secondary color days to begin the dye techniques. By the workshop's end, the students have learned to see the effects of adding black to darken a color, or use the direct complement of a color to dull the existing color. I teach this way because after the "why" connection is made in color combining, the rest is all excitement.

I encourage you to have a blue, red, and yellow day as you practice. You will be amazed how fast color theory becomes second nature.

The direct complement relationships here are: blue and orange, purple and yellow, then red and green. On the color wheel they are located directly opposite each other.

Wool dyed by former student Ivana Vavakova. This is one of the best examples of color, value and intensity. The textured wool adds a nice variety once it is dyed. Notice how your eye travels to the stark white first, it is the brightest and lightest. The white wool was placed here to see what would happen as the eye looks at the wool. *Courtesy of Ivana Vavakova.*

Complementary Colors

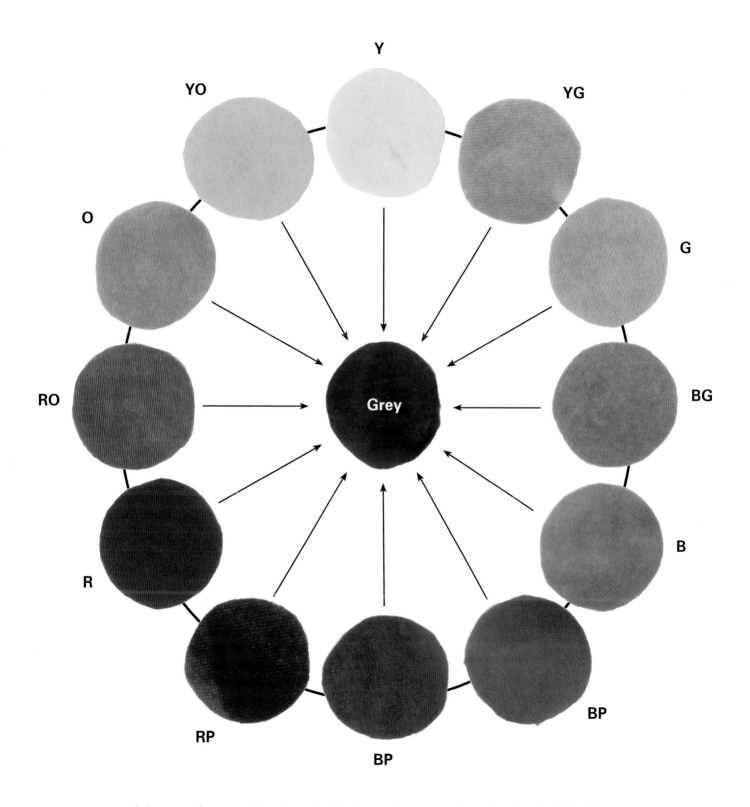

A direct complement sits directly opposite from its complementary color on the color wheel. By mixing different amounts of dry dye powder in direct complement colors, the colors will dull each other. *(Powell, 1984, 24)*

Level of Value of Pure Color

Warm Colors

Cool Colors

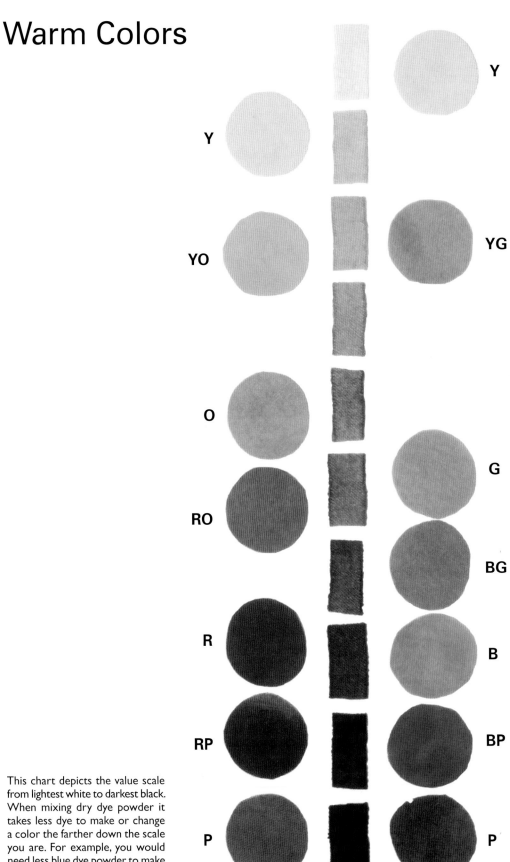

This chart depicts the value scale from lightest white to darkest black. When mixing dry dye powder it takes less dye to make or change a color the farther down the scale you are. For example, you would need less blue dye powder to make a medium value color than yellow dye powder. *(Powell, 1984, 15)*

Pro Chem

True

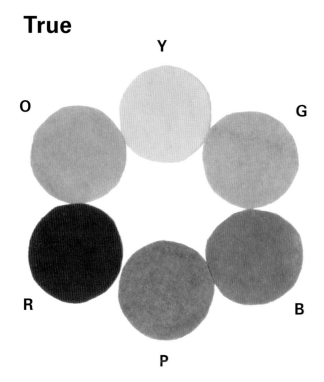

119 Yellow
490 Brilliant Blue
351 Bright Red

Both circles contain primary colors. The left circle has what are considered true primary colors, and the right circle has pastel primary colors.

Pastel

135 Yellow
440 Brilliant Blue
366 Bright Red

The starting hues and intensities differ, therefore the resulting colors will vary in value and intensity. *(Powell, 1984, 9)*

The dyed wool represents both the warm and cool colors on the color wheel. I enjoy having available a variety of values and intensities when mixing colors on a project.

Recommended Wash Fast Acid Dye Colors:

True Primaries:

119—Sun Yellow
351—Bright Red
490—Brilliant Blue

Pastel Primaries:

135—Yellow
366—Red
440—Bright Blue

Other Colors:

233—Bright Orange
338—Magenta
502—Chocolate Brown
503—Brown
672—Black

After you experience the list above I recommend:

817—Bright Violet
818—Violet
478—Turquoise

725—Forest Green
728—Leaf Green

You will find your personal favorites; these are a few basic colors to enjoy.

Warm & Cool

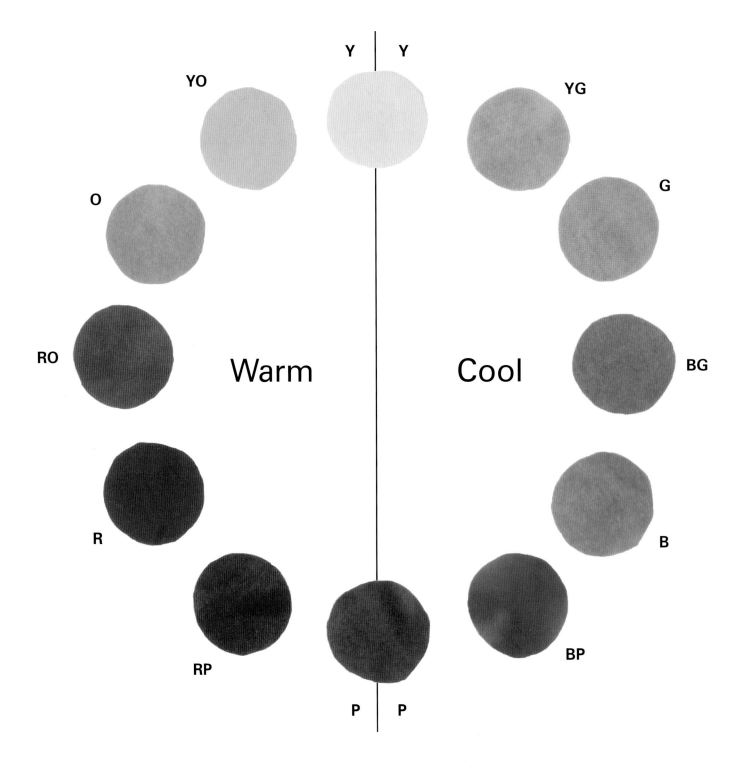

This chart represents the warm and cool colors from PRO Chemical & Dye Inc.® using PRO WashFast Acid Dyes.

Color Sense

There are many colors already made. To develop your own skills, try mixing your own blends. Just play and you will find that to have a variety of colors and textures is more fun. You will eventually use or need the colors you produce.

Note: In the captions of this book I have included many formulas. It is important to clarify how I have written the formula. I have introduced the name of the color once. I then refer to the color's number first, then the measured amount. If you see colors listed parentheses, everything within that parentheses belongs in one beaker.

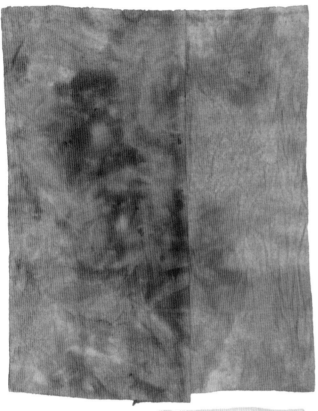

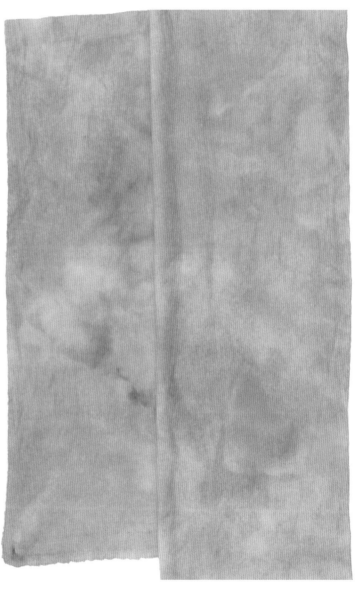

Clockwise from top left:

Overdye Technique: True primary Bright Red [351], is on the left, and the pastel primary Red [366], is on the right. The same amount of dry dye powder and wool was used for each dye bath.

Overdye Technique: True primary, Brilliant Blue [490], is on the left and the pastel primary, Bright Blue [440], is on the right. The same amount of dry dye powder and wool was used for each dye bath.

Overdye Technique: True primary Sun Yellow [119], is on the left, and the pastel primary Yellow [135], is on the right. The same amount of dry dye powder and wool was used for each dye bath.

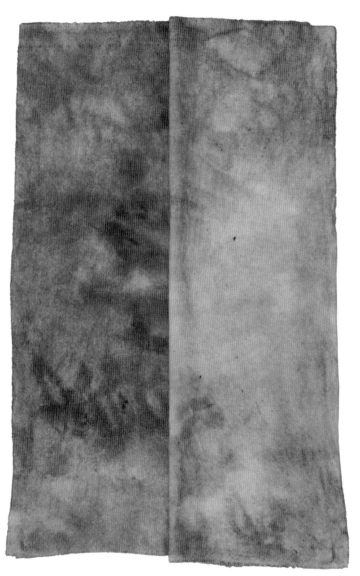

NATURE'S BLEND

Nature blends the primary colors and does an amazing job. I still find myself taking pictures of leaves and flowers as the seasons change in order to reproduce the color palette of nature in the dye pans. Fall reds, oranges, and warm yellows against spring's yellow green and bright purple...wow. The amazing summer sunset may be duplicated in a color transition dye technique. Sunrise and sunset colors are beautiful, ever changing, and one of the easiest places to experience color.

What is your sky color today? In Kentucky's December, I see bright blue, gray blue, and orange blue over the course of several days. Apply this practice to your day, and many good things will come out of the dye pans. The colors in the wool will amaze you when you are done.

Color Overlay Technique: The results on the left show the secondary colors made from the true primary colors. The secondary colors orange, green and purple are a medium value here. The wool swatch on the right is the same technique using the pastel primary colors resulting in a lighter value. The wool amounts and dry dye powder were the same in each dye bath. Due to the strength of the dry dye in the individual hues, this is the perfect example to see the value and intensity difference.

Split Complements

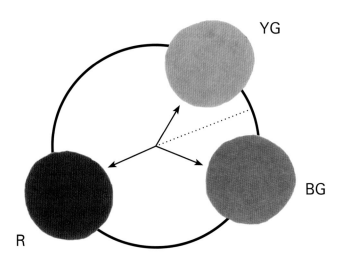

In the split complement relationship a triangle is formed by choosing a color, then using both of the colors on either side of its complement. Both of those colors are split complements. A double complement relationship

Double Complements

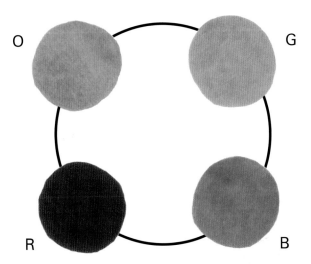

is two colors equal distance apart, and with their complements a square is formed. Both of these relationships may be moved around the color wheel. *(Powell, 1984, 25)*

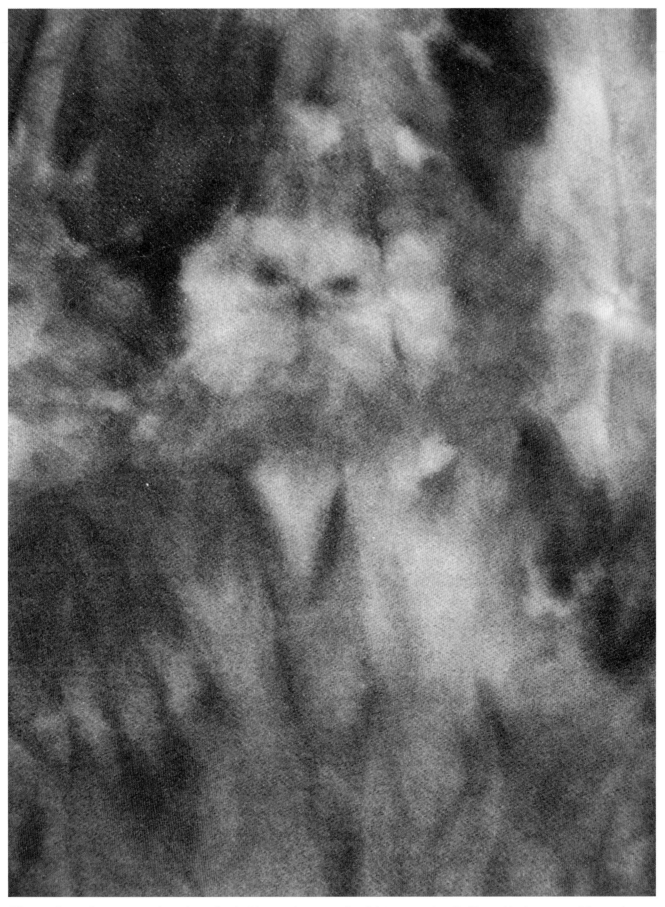

This wool swatch represents the colors of a double complement resulting in red, green, orange, and blue. Celeste Duffy, Holden, Massachusetts, a friend and former student, dyed this wool in class, then left it as a parting gift. The owl in the center of the wool was a surprise, now in my private collection of really exciting wools.

Triad

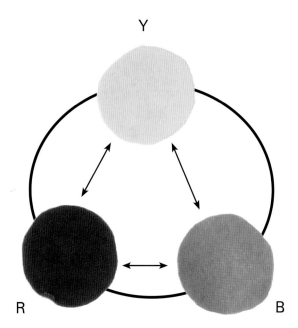

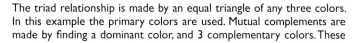

Mutual Complements

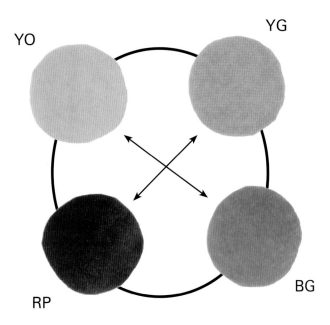

The triad relationship is made by an equal triangle of any three colors. In this example the primary colors are used. Mutual complements are made by finding a dominant color, and 3 complementary colors. These are color planning tools when deciding what colors to dye, and then use in your project. *(Powell, 1984, 26)*

The front center swatch is lightest and contains some of the same colors in the other wools, making this group harmonious. The brown sitting right front is considered a neutral, a place for the eye to rest. The orange in the left front is the dominate color, however the eye treats this as a mutual complement relationship. All of these wools could be used in one project.

Analogous Colors

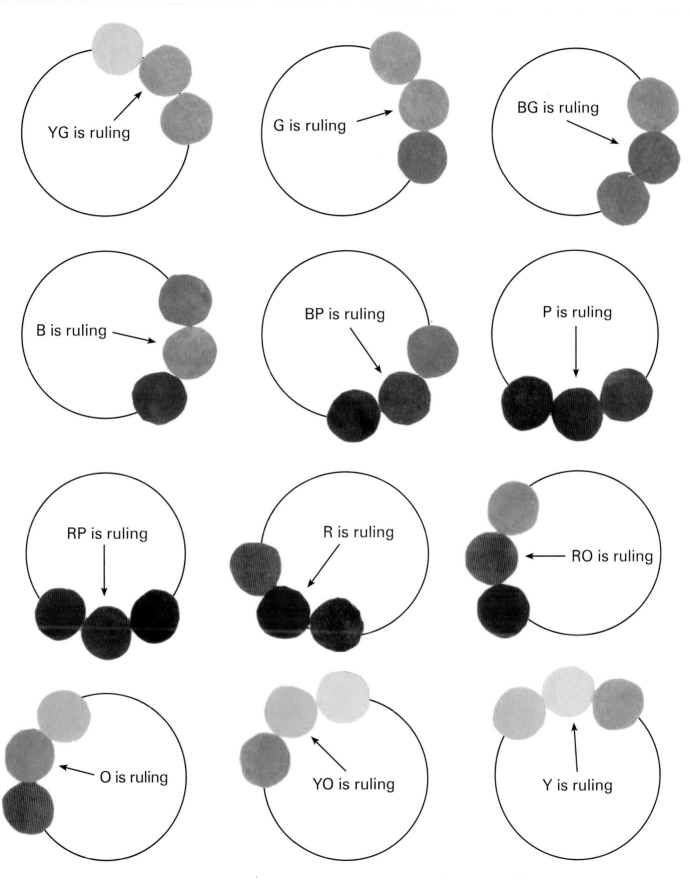

YG is ruling

G is ruling

BG is ruling

B is ruling

BP is ruling

P is ruling

RP is ruling

R is ruling

RO is ruling

O is ruling

YO is ruling

Y is ruling

Analogous colors, adjacent to each other on the color wheel, and may be any value of the color.
This is another color planning tool to achieve color harmony. (Powell, 1984, 28)

This is an example of an analogous color relationship. The colors and values in the textured wools, vibrant reds, purples, and oranges are harmonious.

The original texture in the wool provides added depth and fun. This wool was dyed by former student Ivana Vavakova. *Courtesy of Ivana Vavakova.*

Monochromatic

Purple is the color of choice in this monochromatic (one color) color plan. The lightest to the darkest value, this is a great challenge and perfect for the Jar Dye Technique if doing a smaller project. *(Powell, 1984, 29)*

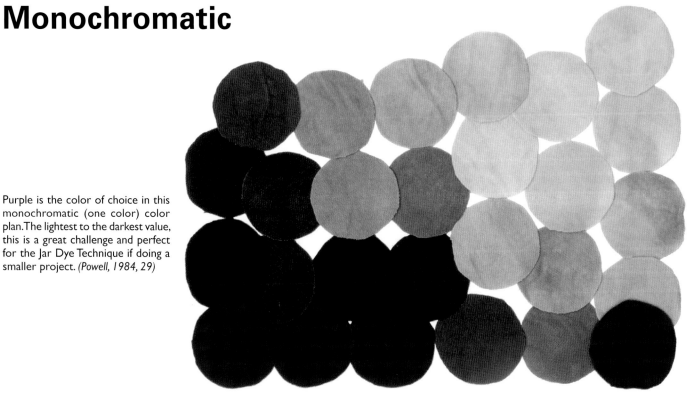

Colors Affect One Another

An example of how one color affects another. The surrounding colors of a hue create a different affect. They may fight or grey each other, play with background colors and see what happens. *(Powell, 1984, 35)*

Color makes you feel a certain way. Focus on one-quarter of the photo at a time and notice the emotions or mood it creates. Hand dyed wool is from my wool stash. *(Powell, 1984, 35)*

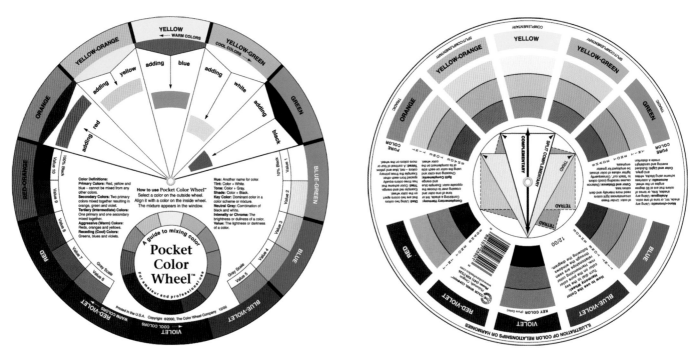

The Pocket Color Wheel™ is the absolute best color wheel I have found when learning how to mix dry dye powder and then to color plan for harmony.

The back of the color wheel offers a wealth of knowledge when color planning, *Courtesy of Ken Haines, President of The Color Wheel Company.*

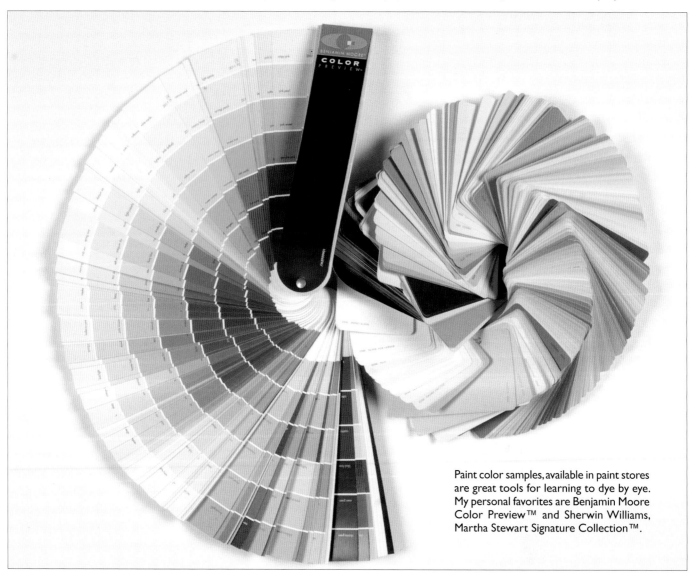

Paint color samples, available in paint stores are great tools for learning to dye by eye. My personal favorites are Benjamin Moore Color Preview™ and Sherwin Williams, Martha Stewart Signature Collection™.

YOU'RE LEARNING LANGUAGE!

CONCRETE OR RANDOM?

According to the Gregoric learning inventory, I am a "concrete random" learner. When learning, I need to see the end goal and then be permitted to find my way to that goal. I avoid using step one, step two, and three; I am frustrated in a structured learning environment. I am also aware I prefer to see a picture or be shown how to accomplish a new task, rather than be told how to do it or be expected to read instructions.

For example, I recently took a wonderful class with a fantastic teacher. I would ask her to "show" me what she was talking about. She would ask each time, "Did you read the instructions?" I would have to say, "No." So, I would skim the words and then ask, "Now will you show me?" I had to do this for every new concept in the class. It was no reflection on her amazing teaching skills; rather, she was more concrete sequential, preferring written words for instruction, such as steps 1, 2, 3, and so on. I prefer to skip steps and be shown.

I supply a notebook to my dye classes, which has become this book. It contains the instructions in written words and pictures. In class, I demonstrate the techniques and every student goes to their station to experience it on their own. If the student needs sequenced steps,

When dyeing wool in a variety of colors and techniques such as these, you will need materials and dye tools. The tools may range from dye pans and glass jars to squirt bottles and rocks, and then some.

I am able to refer to the notebook so the student can move through the exercise with confidence. It is good to know how you learn a new topic; it is empowering, removes stress in a learning environment, and enables us to become lifelong learners.

I have taught this way for years. This year, while the students were unloading their class supplies, I was able to determine their learning style just by looking at how their supplies were organized. I had 3 concrete sequential ladies on the back row and they grounded the other 5 concrete random gals, including me.

WHY DYE?

Over the years, I have seen many students make stunning piles of colorful dyed wool at their desks. The students love the amazing colors they have created. I am never sure if they are excited because they love the color or because they dyed it without a formula. In any event, the excitement is obvious.

MOTIVATION

Motivation comes in many different forms. For me, early in my hooking years I began dyeing my own wool to save money. Dyeing wool does take time and tools, but it is a cost saver in the end.

Creativity is now being used in clinical settings to relieve stress. I work in the world of wellness during the day and, other than exercising for health, I have not enjoyed anything as much as turning on the dye pans and getting creative. There is such a great sense of self-satisfaction knowing the wool you just dyed is going into your project at hand.

I have witnessed tears, joy, happiness, confidence, and many other signs of self-satisfaction in the classroom. It is very rewarding to see the smiles coming from students who now possess skills in mixing colors and understand a wide range of dye techniques. One student expressed her enhanced sense of empowerment and "independence" as a result of learning to dye her own wool. She jumped in the air and clicked her heels together. Every goal in learning to dye wool is a personal one.

For each of us, there are many rewards from the time spent in the dye pans, as the child in us plays with the colors. Life delivers many blows, but, as we manage to keep it together day by day, dyeing a little wool goes a long way!

In April, 2004, my husband was activated into the U.S. Air Force, I had just survived breast cancer surgery, and summer was on its way. That same July, an oak tree crushed our home. We packed everything up and were displaced to an apartment for seven months. Finally, stressed to the limit, I had my dyes removed from storage and, with dye pans on loan from Elsbeth, I dyed wool in the apartment. I dyed wool all day, as if there was nothing left for me to do. The wool had a purpose that day; it was for a cornice project when we returned to our home. It was the best day I can remember from that stressful time, and I could feel the benefits in my body, mind, and soul.

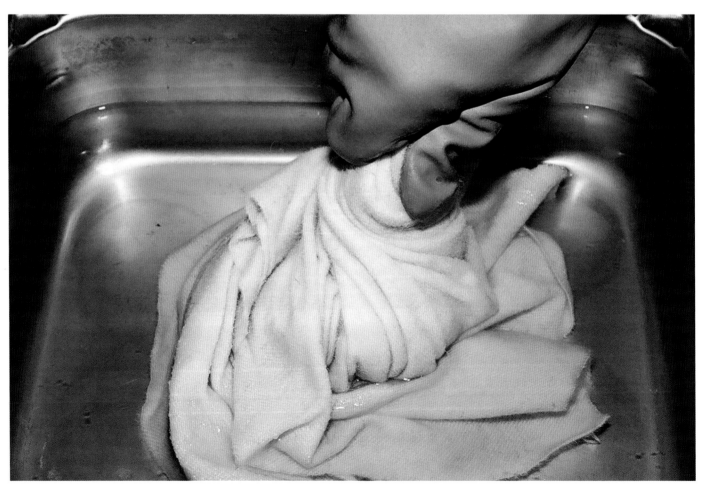

Double Dip & Twist technique, see page 101.

Safety precautions include, on the left, a dental mask, center, Bluettes™ gloves, and, right, dental latex gloves. Safety is a priority when dyeing wool, and dealing with individual health issues. Please be responsible.

SAFETY

At PRO Chemical & Dye®, Lab Support Technician Vicki Jensen answered the following questions pertaining to the safety of their products. Vicki's degree is a Master of Fine Arts and not in chemistry. I respect and follow the recommendations she shares about the dye products used in this book.

As a retired Registered Dental Hygienist, I am aware of safety regulations in place to protect individuals from harm. Common sense must prevail when dealing with any product. I choose to follow any guidelines according to my own health issues. When I retrieve citric acid crystals from my big container and transfer them to my small jar I put on my dental hygiene mask. I know what works for me and I honor the extra steps it takes for me to be comfortable.

I only wear the Bluettes™ brand gloves in the hot water. I measure the dry dye powder into a beaker, add a small amount of hot tap water in the bottom of the beaker to create a paste, then immediately recap the dye jar. Only then do I return to the beaker and add more boiling water to dissolve the dye powder. Consider first your personal comfort level as you use the products as recommended by PRO Chemical & Dye Inc®.

If you turn the cuff down an inch or more on your Bluettes™ glove it prevents water running down your arm as you dye your wool.

Conversations with Lab Support are scattered throughout the book when a particular topic arises, and these are in the Q&A format.

Q: When preparing the dye bath, is the wash fast acid dye toxic? If so, what do I do to prevent exposure?

A: Dyes are not toxic unless you are exposed to them under severe conditions, such as inhaling or ingesting a whole jar of dye. Wearing a white disposable respirator is your best precaution to avoid inhaling any airborne dye powder.

Q: Should I wear a mask all of the time or does it depend on how much wool I dye?

A: You should always wear a mask when working with the dry dye powder. Once it is a solution, you no longer need to wear it.

Q: What if an individual has compromised respiration?

A: Use a mask while mixing dyes and have good ventilation.

Q: What about citric acid and septic tanks?

A: If you dye infrequently, 2-3 pots in a day, there should be no problem. The color is exhausted and there is no dye agent left in the pot when it goes down the drain. If you are concerned, remove the wool and then use baking soda in the pot. Baking soda neutralizes the pH. You can purchase pH strips to test the acid level and continue to add soda to reach a pH of 7.

Q: What about the citric acid safety?

A: You are not using enough citric acid to make a difference in your drains or septic tanks; you are using food grade citric acid.

USEFUL BITS

The following Information is from the PRO Chemical & Dye Inc.®, gathered from a conversation with lab support discussing general topics.

Q: What does Wash Fast mean?

A: Wash Fast is the owner's trade name for these dyes.

Q: Is the foam the only difference between Synthrapol P and Synthrapol LF?

A: Yes.

Q: What type of pan is recommended to dye wool with the Wash Fast Acid Dyes?

A: All acid dyes should be used in a stainless steel or enamel pan.

Q: In the past, I have used aluminum foil and citric acid, and noticed the foil breaks apart. I also know if I leave leftover dye water with CA crystals in the pan overnight pin holes are created in the pan. Is this result from the citric acid on the aluminum?

A: Yes.

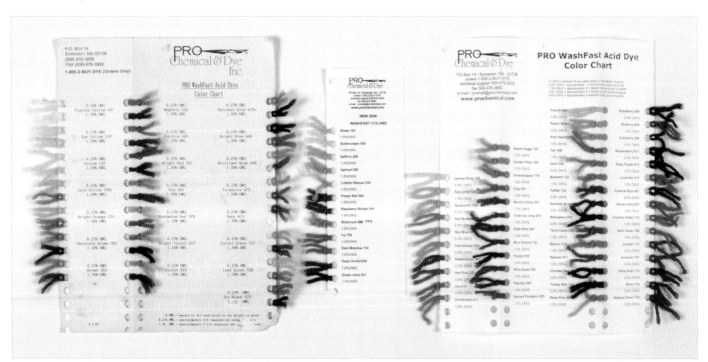

PRO Chemical & Dye Inc.®, Pro Washfast Acid Dye Color Charts, these are available through the company. See resources. *Courtesy of Pro Chemical & Dye Inc.®*

In my experience I have found that if I wash each dye pan with soap and water at the end of the dye session, no harm comes to the aluminum pans. I will, however, eventually replace all my pans with stainless steel.

If the goal is to boil water, a roasting pan is not the best choice. High quality roasting pans are made from a combination of metals to inhibit the boiling process. A roasting pan is typically used in the oven, where the heat is distributed around the pan, and therefore the meat, and the pans contents are not meant to boil.

Q: What is PRO Chemical Company's recommendation for dyeing wool in the microwave?

A: PRO Chemical & Dye does not endorse microwave dyeing.

My one and only experience with dyeing wool in the microwave resulted in a fire. I only heat water and cook popcorn in our microwave. I prefer to follow the guidelines set forth with the Pro® Wash Fast acid dyes.

DYE LANGUAGE

Dye language is not difficult. For clearly understanding and applying the lessons in this book, however, I want us to speak the same language. All crafts have their own particular names for tools, and skills, and the same applies here.

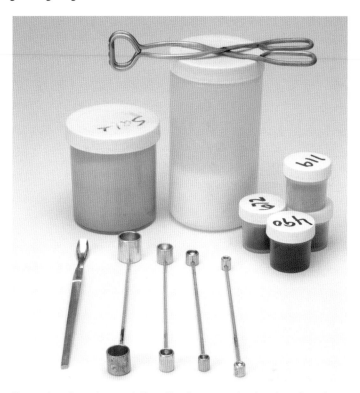

Essential tools to dye wool: Grey Dye Spoons in the 4 pack or 3 pack, my favorite antique tea spoon to stir the dye bath, tongs, dry dye powder, salt, and Citric Acid Crystals, (CA). This is the most basic set up for dyeing wool.

The **dye bath** is the cup that contains the dry dye powder and boiling water. Once the dry dye is in the beaker, add tap water to make a paste, and then add boiling water to dissolve the dye powder. The terms "dye bath" and "color" will be used interchangeably when discussing a technique.

Plastic beakers, available in 1 cup and 4 cup sizes, are perfect for dissolving the dry dye powder with boiling water. *Courtesy of Pro Chemical & Dye Inc.®*

This is how my dye station looks in my studio. I have one table dedicated to the mixing of the dyes, with plastic dental trays. The jar of salt is used to prevent any cross contamination of dry dye by stirring the spoon vigorously in the salt after each use. Note the wool fabric under the mixing station to catch spills.

The **dye pan** is the pan on the stove that holds the water, wool, dye, and citric acid crystals. The size of the dye pan will vary according to the specific technique. Each technique discussion covers this in more detail.

The **stew pan** is a second pan filled approximately two-thirds full with water, and one tablespoon of citric acid crystals dissolved in the pan. The pan is placed on a stove with heat. This pan provides a place for your dyed wool swatch to rest as you continue to dye wool in the dye pan. The purpose of a stew pan is to start the setting process and to separate swatches as you continue dyeing.

A **wetting agent** is a surfactant that opens wool fibers to allow water to soak in by removing any sizing agents in the fabric. It may be added to the soak bucket or directly into the dye pan. I use Synthrapol from PRO Chemical & Dye Inc.®; however there are other brand name products to accomplish this step.

Synthrapol is also used at the end of the dye process to remove excess dye. It does not "open" the core fibers to allow dye to enter; it merely wets the wool and removes any sizing agents from the wool. Almost every technique recommends pre-soaking wool for a minimum of 30 minutes in water and Synthrapol.

A **setting agent**, citric acid (CA), may be used instead of vinegar. This is the agent that works like a carrier to bring the dye into the wool. Citric acid crystals are dissolved and used at different times depending on the technique. It is the citric acid crystals that set or lock the dye into the wool with proper time and temperature.

It takes approximately 1 tablespoon of CA crystals to one pound of wool. Naturally, there are some variables on how to estimate wool weight, but, as a general guide, one pound of wool is equal to a little over a yard of wool. Typically, I will use 1 tablespoon of CA crystals in each *dye pan.* I may divide the crystals between the dye bath and the dye pan, but the total is 1 tablespoon per pan and this is my comfort level without waste.

The dye technique you are using will determine when to use the setting agent. For example, if I were to use a Paisley Dye Technique I would pre-soak my wool in Synthrapol and CA crystals for a minimum of 30 minutes, though I prefer overnight. If I am using

You're Learning Language!

This is the old wool swatch used under my mixing station to catch any spills while mixing dyes. There is no mess to clean up and the results are always a surprise. The wool may be used later in a project after proper setting in CA crystals.

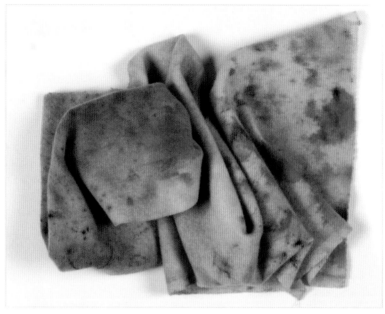

This is the same swatch. Spills become rewards when this swatch is viewed as if it were being used in a traditional hooked rug.

This wool was used to remove color from the dye pan during a technique. The wool is set by the standard setting process. It becomes an added pearl in the wool stash.

Cadco Ltd. Burner. If you do not have access to a stove I have found this burner to be the most dependable and efficient for dyeing wool in a portable situation. It comes in a variety of price ranges and may be found online or restaurant supply stores.

A 4-inch half hotel pan, available at restaurant supply stores, is available in stainless steel or aluminum. I prefer the stainless steel version. The 4-inch height prevents arm fatigue when dyeing different techniques.

The old enamel refrigerator drawer can also be used to dye wool, but they are difficult to find. Both the hotel pan and the white enamel allow you to see the true color.

an Over Dye Technique, I may put the CA crystals in the dye pan first, then add the color and the wool. In this technique, I could also wait much longer before adding the CA crystals.

If I have more than one color going onto the same piece of wool, the CA crystals are used at the beginning of the technique to keep the individual colors visible in the wool. By adding the setting agent at the beginning of the process, the colors go into the wool faster and create a more mottled affect. The citric acid crystals are the key to avoiding "mud" when you are working with several colors on one wool swatch.

Salt is a **leavening agent** to give a smoother appearance to the dyed wool; it does not set the dye into the wool. There are several different salts on the market. While sea salt differs from table salt, I fail to see a discernible difference in my dyed wools when I use one rather than the other. Glauber Salt is another kind of salt available, recommended for light values.

IT MATTERS WHEN IT MATTERS

"It matters when it matters" is a term I use to bring attention to several critical points about the process of dyeing wool.

What is my goal and how do I get there? These are the basic questions to ask yourself as you dye wool. The following concepts will help you understand what is occurring in the dye pan. It will also clarify why certain steps are critical to the results in one technique and not in another. This is the area where my concrete traits are put to use, while my random traits are used when the color is placed on the wool.

If you decide to have 3 different blues in one dye pan on one piece of wool and the CA crystals are not in the pan, the three different blues will become one new blue color. The three individual blue colors are made in separate beakers and the citric acid crystals needs to be in the dye pan first.

This same concept works with values. What if you want to dye a piece of wool with a light, medium and a dark, bright red color in the same pan? The CA crystals need to be in each beaker, to keep the values separated.

If the goal is to have the same or different colors go into the wool and keep their individual identity, CA crystals are necessary at the beginning of the process and they may be in the individual beakers, in the pan, or both.

If the dye pan is already heating on the stove, you may use that hot water to dissolve your dry dye powder. If you are alone in your dye kitchen, it is better to have made a strong dye solution. I find it is better to

Most restaurant supply stores will offer a variety of stainless steel pans in all shapes and sizes that may be used for different dye techniques.

have the dye there, and not need it rather than need more color and not have it.

In the techniques, unless otherwise stated, salt is optional. Remember salt will soften the appearance of color on the wool in a light or medium value. When the directions state that it is optional, feel free to use salt in your dye pan.

When washing the wool at the end of the process, I use dish detergent. The soap removes any residual citric acid in the wool. I place a pan in the sink, squirt a little dish detergent, hand wash, and then rinse the wool. If you decide to use a washing machine, the rinse-only cycle does not remove the citric acid. In warm weather, I prefer to line dry. In the winter, I will use the dryer on low heat with a towel.

There are many wool vendors from which to choose. I love the hunt when shopping for recycled wool, but time is too limited. Once a year I visit, The Dorr Wool Store, in Guild, New Hampshire, and shop. I reward myself when it comes to wool.

A friend of mine has a walk-in closet with shelves stacked full of wool. It is easy to find wool. While I was preparing to be a vendor at the ATHA Biennial, my husband noticed that I had hidden my wool in plain sight. I just smiled.

I refer to a ***motif*** in several dye techniques. Simply put, it is any design item on your pattern. Certain dye techniques require exact measurements when dyeing a width or length of wool for a motif. Once you master the color mixing skills, this measurement would not be so critical; you would simply reproduce any amount of wool necessary.

DYE BY EYE

To "dye by eye" is to dye wool visually rather than using formulas. This type of dyeing is built on training your eyes to see the colors, but it takes experience. It is like making a pasta sauce and not using a recipe. With experience, you can taste it along the way and add ingredients accordingly. You can learn to "dye by eye" in a similar manner, which is why I highly recommend experiencing each of the "color days" within the chapters. Once you have gone through the lessons of color and begin mixing the colors together without a formula, it will become easier to know what to expect as you dye your wool.

You will learn how strong blue is and why you like your red to be more red-blue than red-orange. This skill allows you to reproduce color. I had one student bring a sample of lichen, a beautiful golden yellow, and she wanted me to develop a formula by looking at the lichen color. She observed as I added yellow and brown to match her sample, while taking notes. When she was satisfied with the color, she had a formula to reproduce the color. There are many advantages to learning to dye by eye, and duplicating color is an important one.

There is a great freedom and individuality in having your own color voice. Give yourself time to learn if you are not familiar with dyeing your own wool. Go slow at first and experiment.

Condiment bottles with 1 teaspoon dry dye powder dissolved in boiling water. These sit on the stove top in a pan and are used for minor adjustments when making a color. The bottles contain the true primary colors [490], [351], and [119].

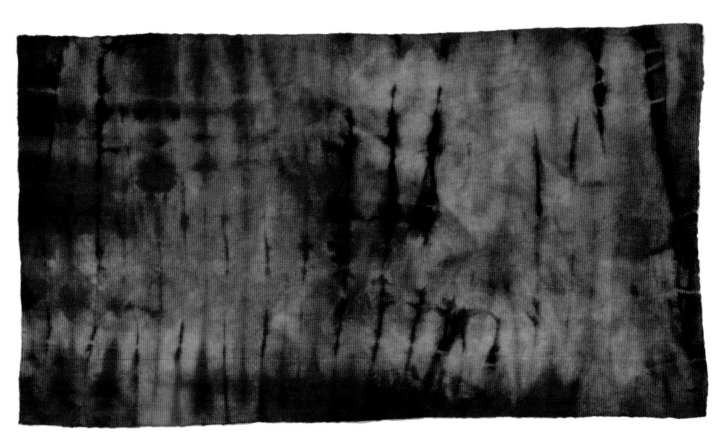

Shibori folded technique demonstrates the results of using only the condiments bottles to dye wool. [490], [351], and [119].

Double Dip Dye Technique: grey, natural and celery wool. The original wool colors play a key role when adding a dye color. Create greater variety by using all three in one project.

THE ZEN
OF DYEING WOOL

This chapter discusses the elements of fire, water, dye, and everything else we must consider in order to have stress-free dyeing. I will include some of the questions and answers from PRO Chemical & Dye Inc.® lab support technician.

FIRE

When using the Pro® Wash Fast Acid dye you need to simmer, without boiling, the dye, wool, water, and CA crystals together in the pan, for one hour. One hour at this constant temperature is the amount of time required for the dye to enter the core fibers of the wool. If the time is less than the recommended one hour, the dye will merely sit on top of the wool. The core fiber cannot be seen with the naked eye according to the lab support technician.

Q: **Why is so important to heat for one hour, rather than just see the clear water in the pan with the dye in the wool, and be done?**

A: To be sure that the dye goes into the very center of the wool fibers.

The purpose is to have the color stay *in* the wool fiber, not *on* the wool fiber, to ensure the color's staying power for a lifetime. Chemistry was not my strongest subject, so every year after returning from the Vermont dye workshop I call the lab support technician, with more questions. I always "go to the source," and I recommend you do the same if you have any doubts about any products.

Although there was no available data concerning the exact temperature the different dyes move into the wool, in my own experiment I found the following: Brilliant Blue went into the wool at 180°F; Bright Red went into the wool at 180°F and Sun Yellow at 182°F. If you choose to do your own experiment, a meat thermometer that attaches to the side of the pan will help, .

When dyeing with blended colors, the color order, in which the dye goes into the wool, is the following: greens, purples, reds, blues, and yellow, which is always the last to leave the pan.

The dyed wools in my studio are shelved and organized in primary colors with their appropriate direct complement and secondary color adjacent to them. This offers additional color lessons to my students. This wool, with the exception of recycled wool, is from the Dorr Mill Store, and includes English and Dorr Wool.

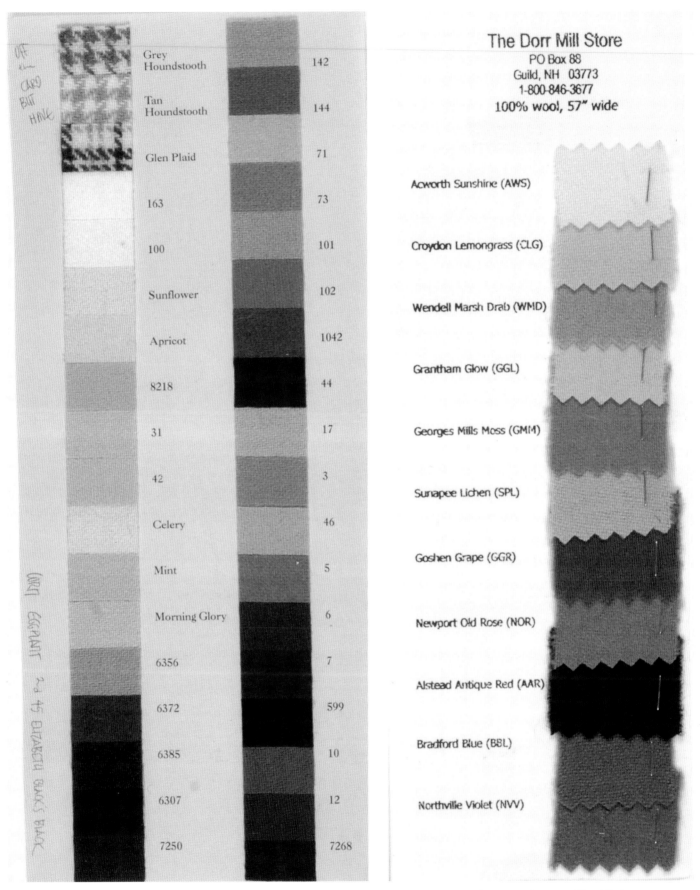

Dorr Wool color chart. Seventy yards of wool was donated by Terry Dorr for this book project. *Courtesy of Dorr Wool.*

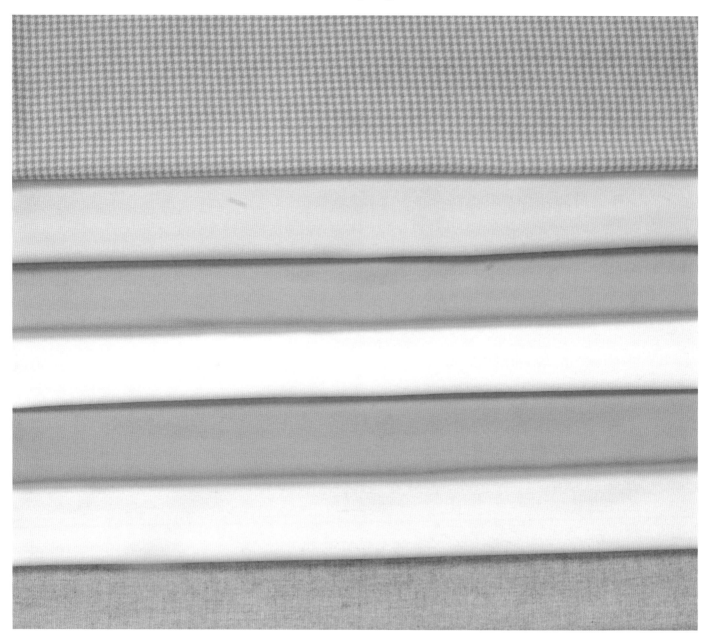

Wool varieties, starting at the bottom: Oatmeal, Natural, 63 Tan, White, 8216 Grey, Sunyellow, and Tan hounds tooth. Celery wool is not shown. *Courtesy of Terry Dorr.*

This knowledge is important when deciding which colors to mix, and what results you may have at the end of the process. For example, if I make green by mixing blue, and yellow, the blue dye may go into the wool first and yellow linger behind a bit. I might conclude this is not the color I expected and add more dye. In class, this is where I stress the importance of time, temperature, and patience. This is worth repeating, time, temperature, and patience.

When adding more dye to a process already started, the one hour clock in "time and temperature" starts over. The one hour time period actually starts when the last dye is added to the pan, be it at the beginning, middle, or end of the technique.

In order for the dye to enter the wool it requires heat at a particular temperature. When dyeing my wool, I keep the water as hot as possible without boiling. Boiling wool will felt or thicken the fabric and this is not my desired goal. I prefer to temper the water as the wool goes into and out of water during the dye technique.

If a piece of wool is taken from one extreme water temperature to another, it shocks the fabric, and may cause undesired results. For example, taking a cold, pre-soaked, wool swatch and placing it into a very hot dye pan would be extreme. The other extreme would be to take the wool from the hot dye pan at the end of the process and wash it under cold water. If felting is desired, the extreme temperatures will start the process.

Dyeing over a textured pattern provides an element of interest and also produces a less intense color. *Courtesy of Pat Cross.*

Always consider the value of the starting wool, and the strength of the dye bath. Textured wools perform as well as solids when dyeing, but the goal depends on a number of color issues. *Courtesy of Pat Cross.*

WATER

The topic of water covers pre-soaking wool to the final washing of the wool at the end of the technique. As stated before, tempering the water is important unless you want to felt your wool. Also remember that the agitation from the washing machine will thicken the wool fibers.

The following recommendations are made by PRO Chemical & Dye Inc.®, and these are the guidelines I follow. Again, I am truly only random when applying color, the pre- and post- steps are very concrete. Please, decide what is comfortable for you.

Q: If I pre-wet the wool and soak it in CA crystals, do I need to apply more CA crystals to the wool in the dye pan?

A: No.

Q: Is there a specified amount of time necessary to pre-wet wool prior to the application of dye going into the wool?

A: A minimum of 30 minutes.

Sometimes I place the wool directly into the dye pan with Synthrapol and bring the water to temperature. By the time I have my color made and I am ready to dye, 30 minutes have passed. So try following this recommended guideline.

Q: Does all water affect the dye colors the same?

A: When working with the acid dyes I have never seen a problem with water quality.

PRO® WASH FAST ACID DYES

The following information will help you have a grounded knowledge base.

Q: What causes the dyes to weigh differently?

A: Their weight is determined by the way that they are manufactured in places like India and China, from where we import them.

Q: Which of the colors fade the fastest?

A: The purple and blue colors fade first. Bright Violet 817 is the worst.

This example, called "fat quarters," is used in most of the dye techniques. The yard of wool starts with one fold and two selvages together, folded lengthwise. The bottom half is folded to the top half so that all of the folds are on the right side and all of the selvages are on the left. The folds are snipped with scissors, then the fabric is torn to create 4 fat quarter swatches.

There are a couple of ways to tear the wool. One yard of wool has a folded edge, and two selvage edges. This example shows the "fold to selvages" fold. With scissors snip the folds tear lengthwise. This provides 4 quarter yard swatches.

Q: Why do the reds have residual color release after setting?

A: They shouldn't, if the dye is applied properly. No color should ever come out of dyed wool.

Q: When working with the Wash Fast Acid dyes are there any tips for deciding whether to add dry dye to water or add water to dry dye when making the dye bath?

A: Adding boiling water to the dry dye powder is the rule of thumb. Occasionally, a color will not dissolve properly, at which time you need to start over and add the dye powder to the boiling water.

Q: If I use the true primary colors to make a secondary color, will the green I make behave differently in the dye pan than the pre-made Leaf Green [728]?

A: Possibly, due to the ratio of the primaries in the mixture and their rate of attaching to the wool.

AND EVERYTHING ELSE

Some other bits of information related to dyeing wool and using the products.

Q: What is the job of the CA crystals?

A: To adjust the pH of the dye bath so that the dye will bond chemically with the fiber.

Q: If I use vinegar with a lower concentration of citric acid than the pure CA crystals will the color in my wool fade faster than if I had used the crystals?

A: Probably, due to the fact that the optimal pH level was not reached for the dye to bond as effectively.

Q: If I complete a dye technique and want to add more dye, how long should I heat the dye pan and do I need to add more CA crystals?

A: Consider starting again from scratch for best results.

Q: Does the size of the CA crystals change the recommended measure of 1 tablespoon CA crystals to 1 pound of wool?

A: Weighing the CA crystals is the most reliable way to assure that you have the proper amount of acid in the dye bath.

Using a calibrated gram scale, I found one level tablespoon of CA crystals weighs 18 grams.

Q: What is the core fiber?

A: The core fiber is the center of the fiber, sometimes referred to as the inner part of the woven wool fabric.

Q: If I decide to dye roving rather than wool, is the setting time different?

A: No, it is the same process.

IT'S A BLUE DAY

Opposite: This is the interior design of "Our Wedding Rug." Leo and I married on harvest moon in 1993. An original design and my colors came from my stash of dyed wool, a result of these dye techniques. Sandra Brown taught a great class on how to use light and this is my result. *Courtesy of Karen and Leo Schellinger, Louisville, Kentucky.*

A variety of dye techniques using different starting wools. In what may at first glance appear to be all bright colors, there are a relative light, bright, dark and dull in this stash.

HOW STRONG IS BLUE?

rue primary blue in WashFast (WF) acid dyes is Brilliant Blue [490], and a little goes a long way. Blue is lower on the value scale (presented in the color theory chapter), therefore less BLUE dye is needed to make a color change.

I can expect to have a light value if my dye measure is 1/32 teaspoon of blue [490] added to the dye pan with a half yard wool. If I begin this process with 1/4 teaspoon of blue, I will have a darker value. The key point here is that you will always be able to add more dye if you need to create a darker value. Using too much blue in the beginning may make the wool a dark value too fast, unless that is your goal.

OVERDYE TECHNIQUE

This is the most basic technique. "Overdyeing wool" is a general term describing dye on wool, but here it is specific to the immersion of the wool into the pan with color or colors added onto the wool already in the pan. When searching for wool to purchase, I consider how it may look overdyed and not necessarily how it looks at the time of purchase.

Right: This stack of blue, purple, and green wool displays various textured dyed wools, a respectable stash for any fiber artist. Wool dyed by former student Ivana Vavakova. *Courtesy of Ivana Vavakova.*

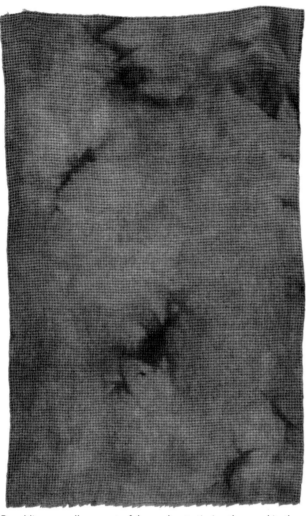

By adding a small amount of dye and not stirring the wool in the dye pan often the original pattern of the wool is still visible. This affect will add interest to any project.

By adding Citric Acid crystals at the beginning of the Over Dye Technique, the wool will have a mottled appearance. Note the original texture still visible.

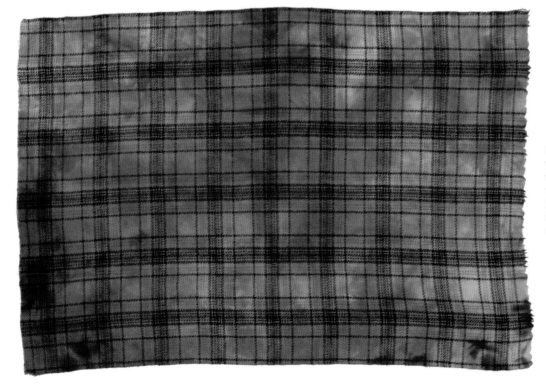

Starting the Overdye Technique with a Glen Plaid wool allows for a darker value overdye. This wool may be used with the wool between the rows for one use in a project and the darker lines for another.

Overdye Technique: In this stack of overdyed wool, the bottom blue is dyed over oatmeal wool, the middle blue is dyed over natural wool, and the top blue is dyed over celery. Same blue dye, different results.

Gather:

- wool, a quarter yard or desired amount, pre-soaked 30 minutes
- 4-inch half hotel dye pan
- beaker
- dry dye powder
- CA crystals
- Synthrapol
- Salt (optional)
- Bluette™ gloves

Start:

- Fill your dye pan two-thirds full of water; simmer without boiling.
- Mix your dye bath by placing the dry dye in the beaker and adding boiling water to dissolve the dye. You may use the hot water in the dye pan for this step.
- Add the color to the dye pan and stir.
- With gloves on add the wool to the pan.
- When the desired value and color are achieved, add CA crystals.
- Simmer, without boiling, for one hour.
- Wash with detergent, rinse well and dry.

1. Pre-soaked wool rests in a second pan while the dye pan water is brought up to temperature. The dye bath is made and ready to go into the dye pan.

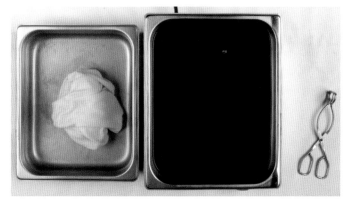

2. The dye bath is added to the pan and brought up to a simmer without boiling. CA crystals are added at the beginning and dissolved.

3. The wool is added to the dye pan, immersed and then either allowed to rest or stirred, depending on preference. Dye, wool, water, and CA crystals now simmer, without boiling, for one hour.

4. After one hour at the simmering temperature, the dye has penetrated the wool fiber instead on sitting on top of the fiber, clear water remains in the pan. Wash the wool with dish detergent, rinse and dry.

Left
Overdye Technique: the increased value changes occur due to infrequent stirring of the wool and/or less water in the dye pan.

Right:
The opposite side of the wool swatch in the previous photo. This shows how the wool would look if the CA crystals were added later in the technique, the change in values are more subtle. Sometimes the prize is on the other side.

 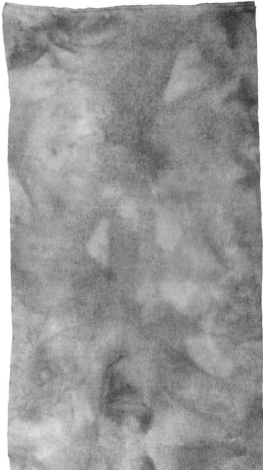

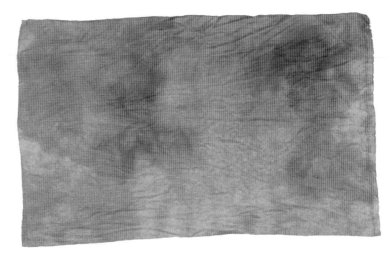

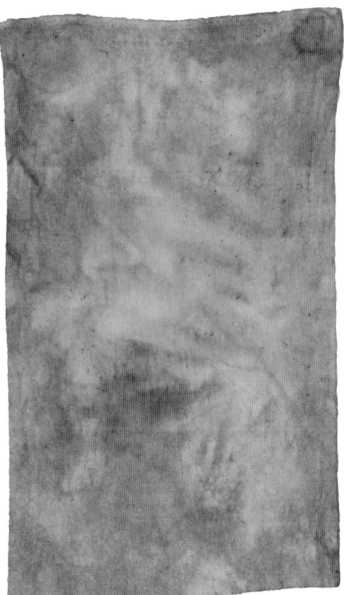

Clockwise from blue: Overdye Technique: One-quarter yard white wool, Bright Blue [440, 1/32], considered to be the pastel primary blue. Increased water in the pan provides a smooth appearance. **Yellow:** Overdye Technique: One-quarter yard white wool, Yellow, [135, 1/16], considered to be the pastel primary yellow. The variation in value is a result of infrequent stirring while adding the dye bath. **Red:** Overdye Technique: One-quarter yard white wool, Red [366, 1/32], considered to be the pastel red primary. Using less water in the pan creates movement in the dyed wool. **Color Blend:** Color Overlay Technique: One-quarter yard, white wool [440, 1/128], [366, 1/64], [135, 1/32]. A close-up reveals the secondary colors orange, green, and purple as a result of bringing together the primary colors in one dye pan. CA crystals are added at the beginning of this technique.

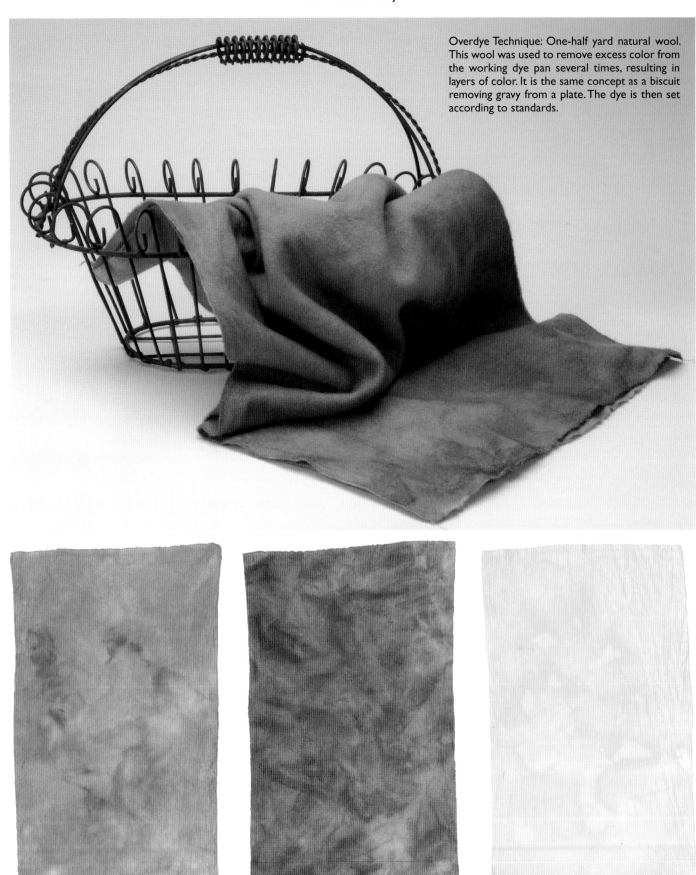

Overdye Technique: One-half yard natural wool. This wool was used to remove excess color from the working dye pan several times, resulting in layers of color. It is the same concept as a biscuit removing gravy from a plate. The dye is then set according to standards.

Left to Right: Overdye Technique: One-quarter yard, white wool, Brilliant Blue [490, 1/32], considered to be the true primary blue, a medium value. Overdye Technique: One-quarter yard, white wool, Bright Red [351 1/32], considered to be true primary red. Some prefer Red [366] as their true primary red; it is a personal choice. Overdye Technique: One-quarter yard, white wool, Sun Yellow [119, 1/32], considered to be the true primary yellow, note the value change from dark to light.

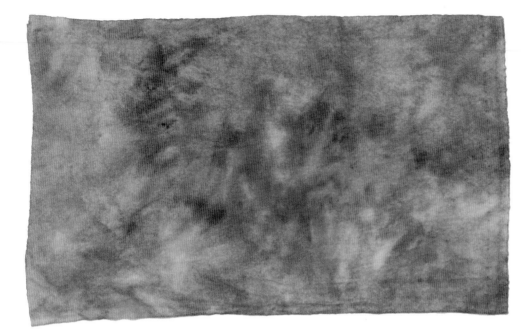

Color Overlay Technique: One-quarter yard, white wool, [490, 1/128], [351, 1/64], [119, 1/32]. The true primary colors in a small amount of dye result in a medium value swatch. The highlights and lowlights occur by using the colors in order of lightest or brightest to darkest color, with dissolved CA crystals already in the dye pan.

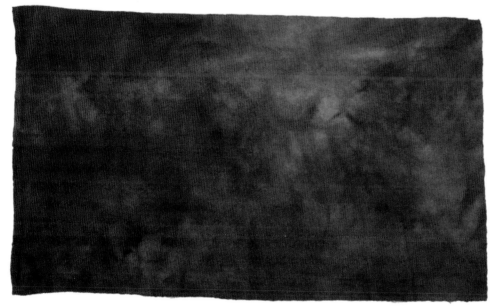

Color Overlay Technique: One-quarter yard white wool, using various amounts of secondary colors, orange, purple and green. True primary colors were used to make secondary colors, then tertiary colors. All of this from three colors!

Adding blue to a light tan wool results in a dull intensity. The changes in value make the color look as if it is dancing on the wool.

Overdye Technique: One-half yard natural wool. Great colors, a result of being used to remove excess dye in the dye pans and then set according to standards. Its always fun to have extra colors around. Two one-of-a-kind pieces.

This textured wool, donated by Pat Cross, was also used to absorb excess dye from the dye pan resulting in an overdye. The wool used for this task usually turns out to be a really great gem, like this one. There is never enough red.

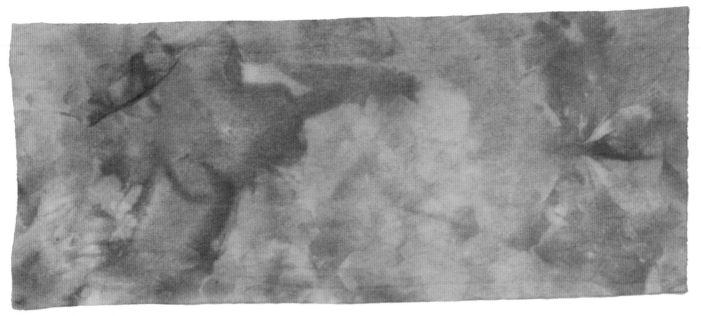

Overdye Technique: One-half yard celery wool, [490, 1/16] + [119, 1/4] placed in the same beaker. A true primary blue and yellow makes this secondary color green. Only one-quarter yard is shown here. Details below.

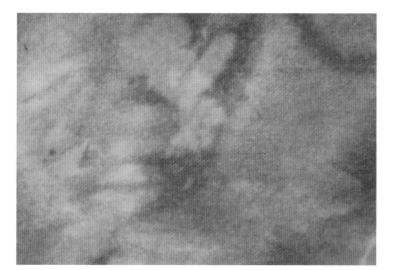

Overdye Technique: One-quarter yard, tan hound's tooth, [119, 1/8+1/16] + [440, 1/128] in one beaker. A true yellow color mixed with a pastel primary blue over textured wool. The textured wool offers built-in movement in a dyed swatch.

Overdye Technique: The solid quarter yard swatches represent a variety of colors dyed with the Overdye Technique. It is always exciting to see the dyed wool together.

DIRECT COMPLEMENT TECHNIQUE

The lesson here is to use direct complements to make wonderful browns. With any direct complement color relationship, it is possible to dye wool from a very light value to a very dark warm brown, with highlights and lowlights. This is the goal of this technique. My favorite combination is orange and blue.

Many of the students in my classes start with very light values and they become so excited they stop the process in the medium value rather than take it to its darkest brown color. Beautiful colors emerge from the dye pans here.

Gather:

- wool, a quarter yard or desired amount, pre-soaked 30 minutes
- 4-inch half hotel dye pan
- extra pan to hold wool
- 2 beakers
- dry dye powder
- 2 colors
- CA crystals
- Synthrapol
- Salt (optional)
- Bluette™ gloves

Traditional hooked rug for a stool to celebrate both the birthday and the gotcha day that Ceci came home from Russia to her new parents. This is a perfect example of a Direct Complement, the name of our next dye technique. *Courtesy of Ceci, Doris and Stuart, Louisville, Kentucky.*

Direct Complement Technique: One yard of natural wool torn into quarter yard swatches. This technique produces marvelous browns at the darkest value. When used together, all direct complements result in a grey or brown; they dull each other. Shown here is the different values that may occur.

Start:

- Fill dye pan two-thirds full of water, simmer without boiling.
- Add the CA crystals to the dye pan.
- Mix the direct complement colors (2) in separate beakers.
- Dissolve dry dye powder with boiling water, stir well.
- Using gloves, place the first and lightest color into the dye pan and stir.
- Place the wool into the pan; be sure the wool is submerged.
- Once the water clears, remove the wool and place it into an extra holding pan.
- Pour the second, darker color into the dye pan and stir.
- Add the wool back into the dye pan and submerge it. This pattern of adding the light color, removing the wool, adding the dark color, then returning the wool into the dye pan will continue until the desired value is reached. When the darkest possible value is reached, I add a very small amount of Black [672] to darken it just a little more. Simmer, without boiling, for one hour. Wash with detergent, rinse well, and dry.

57

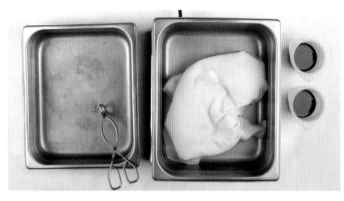

1. Direct complement colors in separate beakers with pre-soaked wool and dissolved CA crystals in the dye pan as the water heats. An extra pan is needed to hold the wool.

2. With gloves on, lift the wool from the dye pan, and pour the lightest color into it. Immerse the wool into the water. Allow the color to enter the wool.

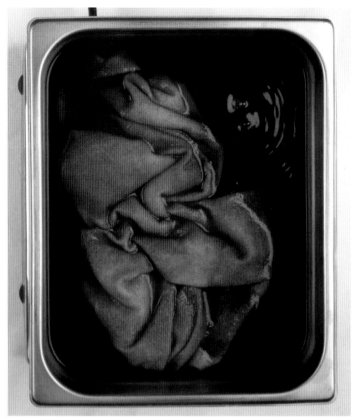

4. As the colors are added and the amount of dye increases the values will change. Students become so excited with the changes they see, sometimes they stop the process and set the color following the standards and do not reach the dark brown. It is hard to dye over yummy.

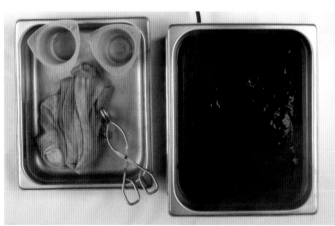

3. Once the water clears, with a gloved hand, lift the wool from the dye pan and set aside. Add the second color to the dye pan. Place the wool into the dye bath, immerse it, and allow the water to clear. Repeat the same steps until your reach the desired value.

When dry the highlights and lowlights are more visible. This translates into movement in the wool swatch rather than a flat solid appearance. This example is a medium value with dark value lowlights.

5. When satisfied with the value of wool as it becomes dull and much darker, you may decide to add Black [672] to darken the value more.

6. Simmer, without boiling, for one hour. The clock begins when the last dye was added. It is fine to add more CA crystals at this time.

7. The water will clear after one hour. Wash with dish detergent, rinse well, and dry.

Direct Complement Technique in a dark value still results in highlights and lowlights. The textured pattern is visible through the warm brown color. Such warm browns...my favorite!

Direct Complement Technique: One-quarter yard, white wool, Yellow [119, 1/128] and Purple [817, 1/128] in separate beakers. Notice the small amount of dry dye used to create the lighter value on a quarter yard of wool. Use limited stirring once the dye is in the pan.

Direct Complement Technique: One-quarter yard, natural wool, [119, 1/64] and [817, 1/64] in separate beakers. Here the dye amount is doubled from the lighter value in the previous photo. This resulted in a medium value of the same color.

Direct Complement Technique: One-quarter yard, natural wool, Yellow [119, 1/16] and Purple [817, 1/16] in separate beakers, then repeated. Once the desired value is reached add Black [672, 1/16]. This photo represents the darkest value of the direct complements yellow and purple.

Direct Complement Technique: The results show Yellow [119] and Purple [817], from light to dark value resulting in a brown/black color. The technique may be stopped at any value desired, because they are yummy.

It's a BLUE Day

Textured wool dyed with direct complement yellow and purple. The added benefit of the original wool pattern is still visible. This technique is great for any value.

This is a really warm brown with a lot of movement. With its darker value, this is a great example of how citric acid crystals keep the colors separated as the dye enters the wool fibers.

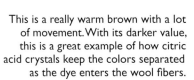

Direct Complement Technique: One Yard natural wool dyed in quarter yard swatches. The direct complement Red and Green will dull each other as shown in each value. Each can easily stand alone or all can be used together in one project.

OPEN PAN VALUE DYE TECHNIQUE

The open pan method is another general term used for dyeing wool. Most of the techniques in this book are accomplished in an open pan. When discussing detailed results, specific names are required to define the relationship of dye to wool for each technique. I refer to the Open Pan Technique specifically to value dye larger amounts of wool.

Gather:

- wool, a quarter yard cut into swatches or desired amount, pre-soaked 30 minutes
- 4-inch half hotel dye pan
- stew pan
- beaker
- dry dye powder
- CA crystals
- Synthrapol
- salt (optional)
- Bluette™ Gloves,

Open Pan Value Dye Technique: Three-quarters yard, natural wool, Yellow [119, 1/4] + Brown [502, 1/32] in one beaker, used as needed. This introduces you to the dye by eye method and is a great way to dye values the same color with larger amounts of wool.

Open Pan Value Dye Technique: three-quarters yard, oatmeal wool, [440, 1/8] + [351, 1/2] in one dye bath. By using oatmeal or a lighter value textured wool, the intensity will be a tone or shade of the original dye color.

1. One holding pan with the pre-soaked wool swatches, one dye pan, and the desired color. CA crystals are dissolved in the pan as the water is brought to temperature. Simmer without boiling.

2. Dye the lightest value first. Place a small amount of color into the dye pan, and then immerse the first wool swatch. The wool may be removed at any time. When you are happy with the value place the swatch in the holding pan.

Start:

- Fill the dye pan two-thirds full of water, add 1 tablespoon CA crystals, and simmer without boiling.

- Fill the stew pan two-thirds full of water, add 1 tablespoon CA crystals, and simmer without boiling.

- Make your color in the beaker, dissolving dry dye powder with boiling water.

- Squeeze the excess water from the swatches, but not too dry.

- Pour a very small amount of color into the dye pan and stir

- Place the first swatch into the pan. This is your lightest value.

- When the desired value is reached, remove the swatch and place it into the stew pan.

- Pour an increased amount of color into the dye pan and stir.

- Place the next swatch into the pan. This is your medium value.

- When desired value is reached, remove the swatch and place it into the stew pan.

- Pour more color into the pan, stir, and place the next swatch into the pan. This is your darkest value. Depending on the size of your swatch once the dark value is reached, I typically leave it in the dye pan. Both pans simmer, without boiling, for one hour. If space is an issue, once the water is clear in the dye pan, all of the swatches may simmer together.

- Wash with detergent, rinse well, and dry.

3. Add more dye to the pan. The wool swatch placed into the pan is the middle value. Again the swatch may be removed at any time. When the value is achieved, place the wool in the available corner of the holding pan.

4. Add more dye to the pan. This will become the darkest value swatch. Process the same, when the water is clear, or in a separate pan with water and CA crystals, simmer, without boiling, for one hour. Keep the swatches separated from each other.

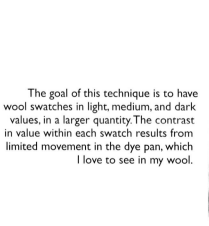

5. One hour later the water is clear and the value swatches are washed with dish detergent, rinsed well, and dried.

The goal of this technique is to have wool swatches in light, medium, and dark values, in a larger quantity. The contrast in value within each swatch results from limited movement in the dye pan, which I love to see in my wool.

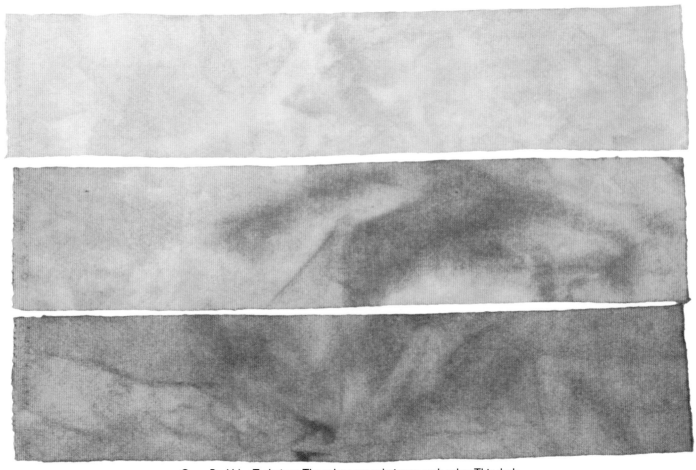

Open Pan Value Technique. The values are relative to each other. This dark value is more medium, but here it is the darkest value of the three.

The top values show a Jar Dye Technique while the bottom wools represent the Open Pan Value Dye Technique. The jars hold small amounts of wool and result in smaller value changes in each swatch.

This warm stash of wool represents the first four dye techniques. The Overdyed gold swatch beside the Direct Complement browns. Red purples from the Open Pan Value Dyeing, and the blues and reds from the Casserole Techniques. These may be blended and mixed together with a variety of color palettes for many projects.

CASSEROLE TECHNIQUE

This technique is very much like cooking lasagna. The results from this technique are just yummy. (I always say, "It's just yummy!" out loud when I see the wools come out of the pan.) In one example for this book, I used leftover dye baths that had been sitting around for the colors in this technique, but the results were not that great. They were too muddy, so I overdyed the wool to something that made me happy.

The color possibilities are endless and always just a little surprising. You can accomplish the Casserole Technique in two ways, with small swatches or with quarter yards folded into the dye pan. I choose the latter because I use wide cut wool strips and prefer longer pieces of wool, although both ways are fine. Colors choices may be analogous, warm, cool, or have other harmonious relationships.

Casserole Technique: Natural wool. If you are unhappy with the original results, everything may be dyed again. In this example I overdyed the entire casserole with Yellow [119]. My theory: if the wool needs a change, add yellow. Now it is just perfect yellow green wool.

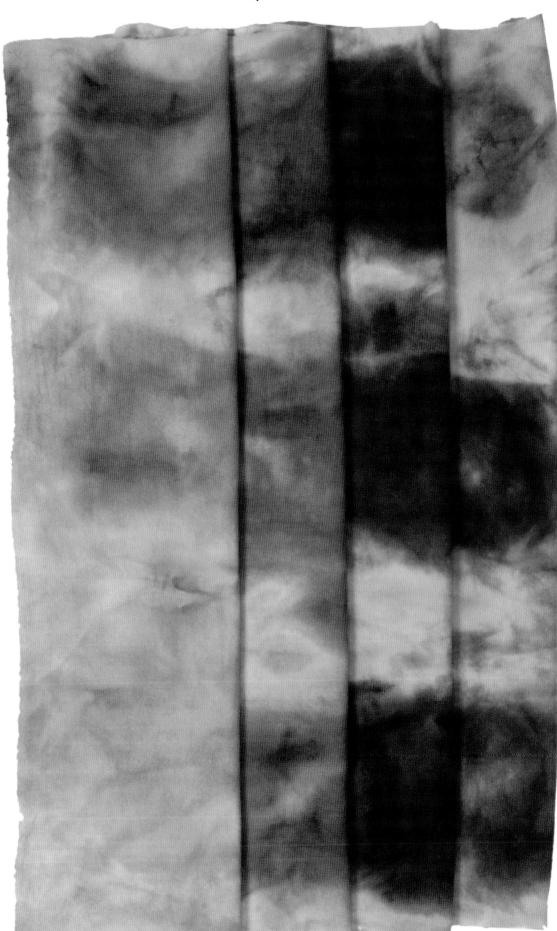

Casserole Technique: One yard natural wool, folded as swatches. Colors used in separate beakers:

[119, 1/16],
[233, 1/16],
[351, 1/16],
[440, 1/16],
[728, 1/16],
[502, 1/16].

The lightest colors are used last or they would be lost under the darker colors.

It's a BLUE Day

1. Casserole Technique: Pre-soaked wool swatches, a dye pan with very little water heating, and 5 to 6 colors with CA crystals dissolved in each beaker.

2. The first swatch is placed in the pan with 3 of the 6 colors being added. Three colors are randomly poured for each layer with salt on top of the wool. Start with the darkest colors first. You may not use all of the color in the beaker.

3. The next swatch is placed on top of the first layer, and three more colors are poured randomly onto the wool. This pattern repeats wool, color, and then salt, except for the last layer of wool.

4. The colors may be used a couple of times prior to adding the next lightest color, 3 colors for each layer. Salt the top of the wool and you are ready for the last layer.

Gather:

- wool, a half yard cut into swatches or two quarter yard pieces, pre-soaked for 30 minutes
- 4-inch half hotel dye pan
- 5 to 6 beakers
- dry dye powder for selected colors
- CA crystals
- Synthrapol
- salt
- Bluette™ gloves

Start:

- Make 5 or 6 colors, each in a separate beaker; add boiling water to dissolve dry dye powder.
- Add 1/2 teaspoon CA crystals to each beaker and stir well.
- Squeeze the water out of the pre-soaked swatches, but not too dry.
- With your dye pan on the counter, place the first piece of wool into the pan bottom. If using longer swatches consider placing a second pan behind the working pan to absorb moisture from the wool as it rests between dye applications.
- Randomly spoon or pour 3 of the colors onto the wool; the colors will overlap. I start with the darker values and work toward the lighter values.
- Salt the top of the wool. If working with smaller swatches, place the next swatch on top of the last. Longer swatches are folded into the pan.
- Using the same 3 colors, pour in random fashion.
- Salt the top and move to the next layer.
- Move darkest color of the three off to the side and bring in another color not yet used.

5. With gloves on, the last layer of wool is gently pressed into the pan, no color is added to the wool. Salt is sprinkled on the top of the last layer. Cover and simmer, without boiling, for one hour. Check the water level in dye pan often.

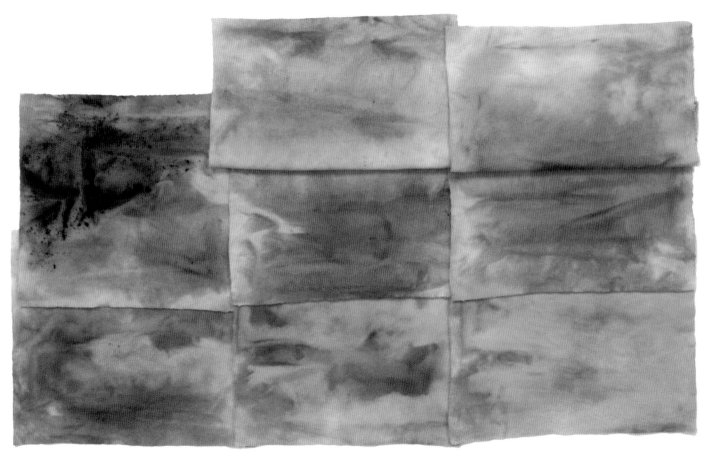

Casserole Technique: Natural wool swatches, [130, 1/16], [135, 1/16], [349, 1/16], Leaf Green [728, 1/16], and [440, 1/16] in separate beakers. This example uses smaller swatches rather than folding the quarter yard swatch into the pan. Both ways yield beautiful results.

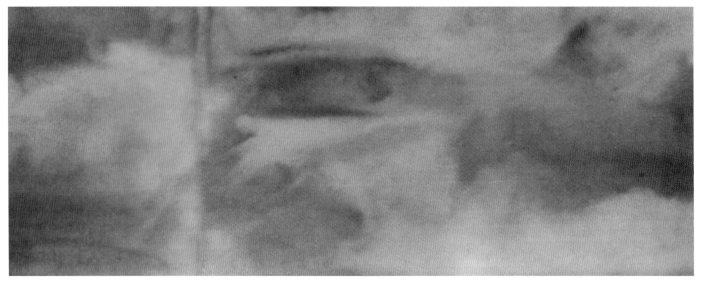

Detail.

- The layers continue in casserole style: wool—color—salt, then repeat in the next layer. Depending on how many layers you are working with, you may repeat colors or move one to the side and pull in another color. You may or may not use the entire dye bath. This continues until there is only one swatch left.

- Place the last swatch on top or fold the last bit of wool into pan.

- With gloves on, simply press the wool gently until the excess dye covers the wool.

- Salt the top layer.

- Dissolve 1 tablespoon of CA crystals into 1 cup of very hot water, then pour the water under the 4 corners of the wool.

- Cover and simmer, without boiling, for one hour.

- Wash with detergent, rinse well, and dry.

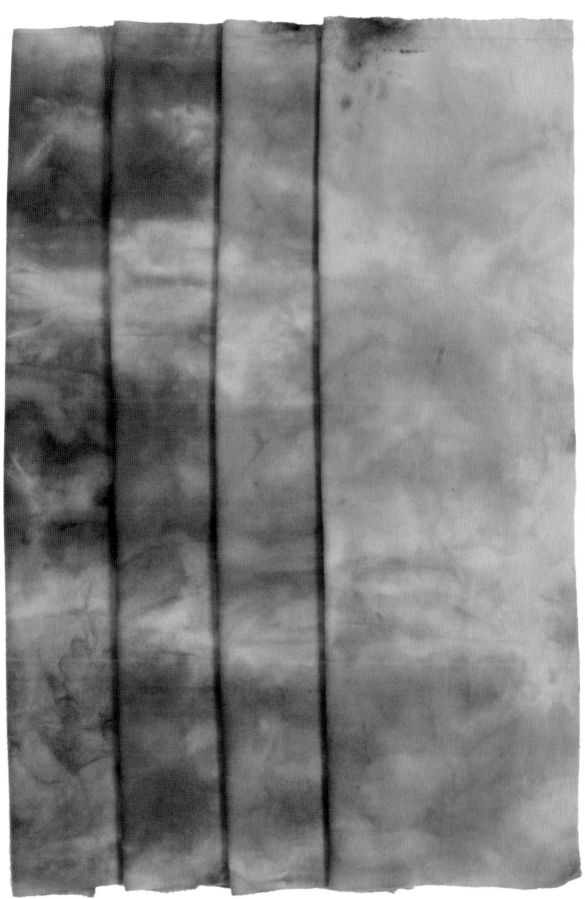

Casserole Technique:
One yard, celery wool,
analogous colors

[440, 1/16],
[725, 1/16],
[818, 1/16],
[672, 1/16],
[478, 1/16]

in separate beakers.
Blues, purple, and
black create an
amazing ocean or
stormy sky. This
shows the quarter
yard not cut into
swatches, but folded.

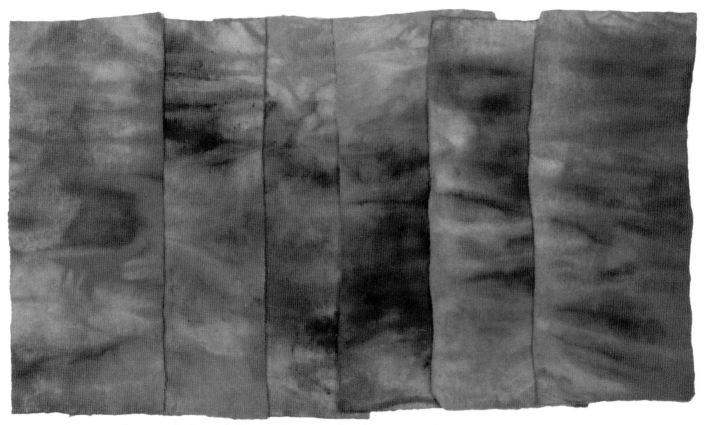

A variety of colors and values resulting in a garden of color, waiting for the next project. This quarter yard was cut into pan size swatches, but the wool may also be folded into the pan, for length.

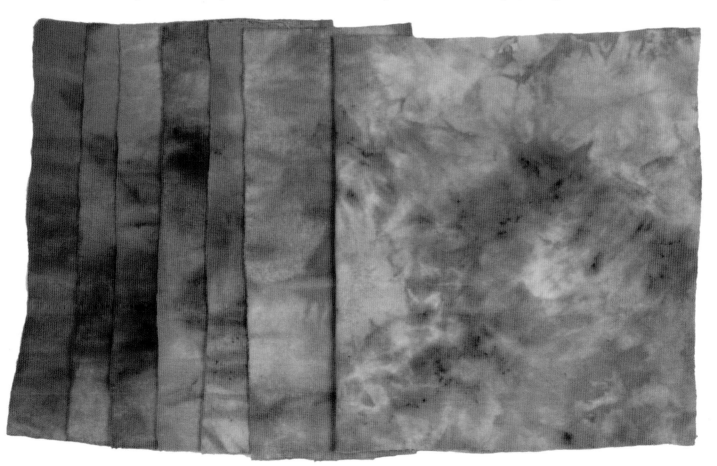

The Casserole Technique swatches on the left simmered in the same pan with the Spot Dye Technique wool on the right. Note the blending of reds. The reds leach out color the most and sometimes it transfers. It is all fine to be used together...an unexpected bonus.

START WITH RED TODAY!

HOW DOES RED FIT?

I refer to use Bright Red [351] as my primary red. Once the dye powder is dissolved, this particular red dye has a habit of looking like spoiled milk; it may clabber. There is no chemical reason offered for this and it causes no damage to the wool in any way. It is recommended that you first put the boiling water in the beaker, then add the red dye powder to the water, rather than adding water to the dye.

Red is in the middle of the value chart, so it will take more dry dye powder to change a color. For a light value on a half yard of natural wool I would measure at least 1/16 teaspoon of dry dye powder. Remember, for the same light value in blue I started with 1/32 teaspoon dry dye powder. Experiment with the strength of red...maybe have a red day. The color red ranges from red orange to red blue, lightest reds to darkest. Play with red and find your favorite.

NORTHERN SPOT DYE TECHNIQUE

This technique was demonstrated to me by Stephanie Ashworth Krauss in Vermont. I also learned a different way to spot dye in the South, so, for clarity in a classroom environment, I nicknamed one Northern and the other Southern. There are differences in liquid volume, but both use 3 to 4 colors in the technique.

Depending on your color and choice in value, the goal of this technique is a blend of color. There will be areas of color that range from intense dark to bright or dull highlights in one piece of wool. Again the possibilities of color and intensity are endless, so just have fun with it.

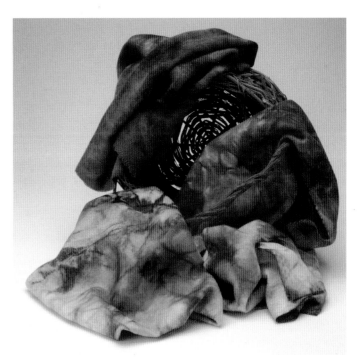

Northern Spot Dye wool in the back top left, and Kettle Spot Dye in front. Notice at the left front, the waffle pattern transferred onto the wool from the metal basket used in the technique. How much fun is that?

Gather:

- wool, a half yard of wool or desired amount, pre-soaked 30 minutes. The goal is to have more wool than pan, like dough falling out of a pie plate.
- 4-inch half hotel dye pan, or 2-inch long hotel dye pan
- 3 to 4 beakers
- dry dye powder for each selected color
- CA crystals
- Synthrapol
- Bluette™ gloves
- salt (optional)

A Southern Spot Dye with soft contrasts and value changes. No two are the same. This is a great way for many colors to be on one piece of wool.

Start:

- Make 3 to 4 colors in separate beakers.

- Add 1/2 teaspoon CA crystals to each beaker, then dissolve dry dye and crystals by adding two-thirds cup boiling water, stirring well.

- Place your dye pan on the counter top.

- Squeeze the water from the wool until it feels paper dry.

- Arrange the wool in the pan by draping it first, so that the wool is open. Start in the middle of the pan and use your fingertips to bring the wool into the pan while creating hills and valleys. Try to avoid an accordion look.

- Pour the first color onto the wool in a tick–tack–toe pattern.

- With your gloved hand, make a fist, hold your arm straight, put your fist on wool, and then lean into your fist. This is the easiest way to disperse the dye without fatiguing your body.

- Continue this pour–press action and retrace your color steps as you empty the first beaker.

- The second color is poured in the same pattern, but it starts between the last colors.

- Continue the pour–press method with the second color.

- The third color is poured in the same pattern, but the main purpose of this (and the 4th color if one is used), is to cover any undyed areas on the wool. If there is a fourth color, use it very sparingly.

- In a beaker, dissolve 1 tablespoon of CA crystals in 1 cup hot water

- Gently pour the water under the four corners of the wool. Cover and simmer, without boiling, for one hour.

Special attention must be given to techniques with little water volume, to prevent the wool from burning, so add water as needed.

- Wash with detergent, rinse well, and dry.

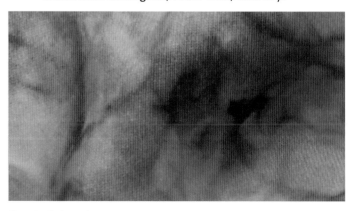

Detail of photo from previous page.

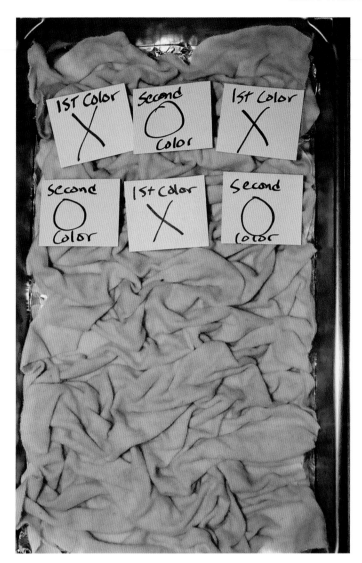

This demonstrates how the wool is placed in the dye pan in both the Southern and the Northern Spot Dye Techniques. Also shown is the tic, tack, toe method of depositing the color onto the wool. Foil in the pan bottom is optional, and shown to give a complete picture. It will break apart due to the citric acid crystals without harm to the wool.

1. Northern and Southern Spot Dye Technique: Open the wool over the pan as demonstrated, then pull it into the pan with fingertips. As the wool enters the pan hills and valleys are created. Three colors are chosen, CA crystals dissolved in each dye bath, and salt. I keep an extra cup of water with CA crystals nearby.

2. The first color is poured or spooned onto the wool in this tick, tack, toe pattern. In the Northern Spot Dye, the color is dispersed into the wool with a gloved hand pressing it into the wool where the color was just poured. Retrace the pattern if there is dye left over.

3. Add the second color between the first, tick, tack, toe pattern. Continue pressing into the color with the gloved hand.

4. The third color is place on any undyed area. Continue the pour and press method to disperse the limited amount of color throughout the wool. Check water level and pour the extra water/CA crystals under each corner of the wool. Set according to standards. This pressing is used in both the Northern and the Spotted Natural Techniques.

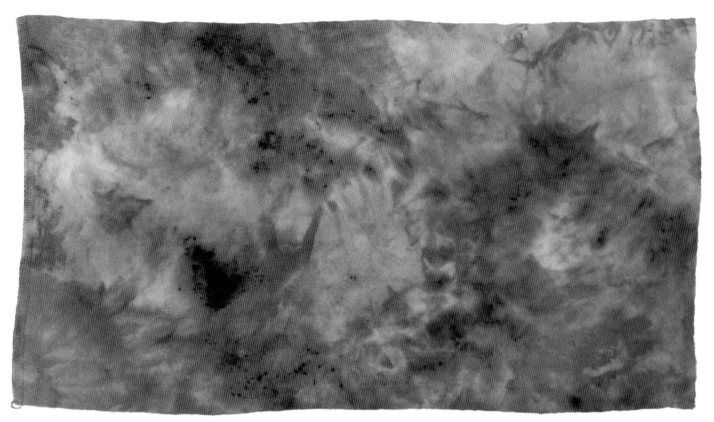

The areas of color intensity are a result of the pressing. There was a very small amount of dye used here and the sharpness in color and intensity is still visible.

The beakers demonstrate the required liquid amounts of color when using the Northern and Southern Spot Dye Techniques. The smaller beakers are for the Northern Technique, the larger beakers for the Southern Technique. This is the major difference in the two techniques.

Northern Spot Dye Technique: Natural wool. Note the many color changes throughout these two quarter yard swatches. The colors and intensity include light, bright, dark, and dull, relative to each swatch.

Northern Spotdye Technique: One-quarter yard natural, left, and one-quarter yard oatmeal wool, right. Leftover blue, purple and orange dyes were used. Note the dark areas of intensity, value changes, and very active movement in the wool.

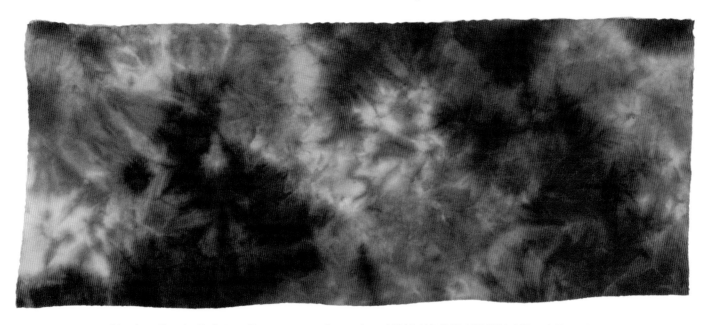

Northern Spotdye Technique: One-quarter yard natural wool, [119, 1/4], [233, 1/8], [351, 1/8], and Chocolate Brown [502, 1/16] in separate beakers. Again, there is great value contrast in this technique.

SOUTHERN SPOT DYE TECHNIQUE

As stated earlier, the only difference between the Northern Spot Dye Technique and this one is the volume of water in the dye baths. This increased water volume in the dye bath will result in a softer blend of color. There may be intense creases in this technique, but that depends on the value of the chosen colors. All spotdye techniques offer amazing results with several values and color intensities on one piece of wool. Refer to the Northern Spot Dye Techniques for picture references.

Gather:

- wool, a half yard or desired amount, pre-soaked 30 minutes. The goal is to have more wool than pan, much like dough falling out of a pie plate.

- 4-inch half hotel dye pan, or 2-inch long hotel dye pan
- 3 to 4 large beakers
- dry dye powder for selected colors
- CA crystals
- Synthrapol
- Bluette™ gloves
- Salt

Start:

- Make 3 to 4 colors in separate beakers.

- Add 1/2 teaspoon CA crystals to each beaker and dissolve dry dye powder and crystals by adding 1 cup boiling water to each beaker and stirring well.

- Squeeze excess water from wool.

- Place your pan on the counter and arrange the wool in the pan by draping it first, so that the wool is open. Start in the middle of the pan and, using your fingertips, bring the wool into the pan while creating hills and valleys. Try to avoid an accordion look.

- Begin by pouring the first color onto the wool in a tick–tack–toe pattern.

- Retrace your steps if you have color left in your beaker.

- The second color is poured in the same pattern, but it starts between the first colors.

Left: This is an example of the proper hills and valleys in any spot dye. Avoid making fan like rows in this technique. The aluminum foil is optional to prevent burning the wool. The CA crystals cause the foil to disintegrate however causes no harm to the wool.

Southern Spot Dye Technique: Natural, oatmeal, celery and white wools. Wow, a great combination of analogous warm colors, blending these together would add great interest and texture to any project.

In the Southern Spot Dye Technique, the salt is added to the top of the wool. I learned to "salt like a roast." The salt helps to "increase a color's yield," according to the dye company. The value changes are more subtle due to more water in the dye bath.

- The third and the fourth colors (if one is used), are poured onto any undyed areas on the wool. Use both sparingly.

- In a beaker, dissolve 1 tablespoon of CA crystals in 1 cup hot water, dissolve crystals, and gently pour under the four corners of the wool.

- Sprinkle the salt on top of the wool and, with gloves on, place your palms open on the wool and gently press only once in each area.

- Cover and simmer, without boiling, for one hour.

- Wash with detergent, rinse well, and dry.

Southern Spotdye Technique: One-quarter yard celery wool. Colors: [119, 1/4], [233, 1/8], [351, 1/8], [502, 1/16] in separate beakers. Stronger dye baths with one yard of wool result in this medium value.

Southern Spotdye Technique: One-quarter yard white wool. Leftover colors: blue, orange, and brick red in separate beakers. A stronger dye bath creates a sharper contrast in values. There is a great variety to these color combinations and many surprises come from this technique.

A green star from, "Groovie Graffiti," designed and hand hooked by Chris Rabeneck. Take time to play with mixing primary colors both in the dye pan and in your projects. *Courtesy of Chris Rabeneck.*

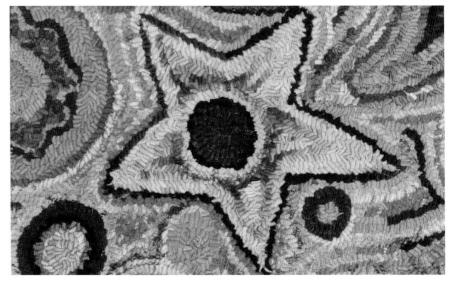

KETTLE SPOT DYE TECHNIQUE

I used to dye wool in an electric kettle that came with a wire basket. I stopped dyeing with the kettle, but kept the basket. When I dye wool using this technique, sometimes the basket pattern is transferred onto the wool, providing extra texture to the finished product.

This year my students took it upon themselves to make baskets using aluminum foil. They even molded handles for their foil baskets, then poked holes into the foil for the water to drain. These baskets worked very well. Bravo ladies.

Gather:

- wool, 2 quarter yard swatches or desired amount, pre-soaked 30 minutes.
- a wire basket with handle or a pasta strainer with holes
- 4-inch half hotel dye pan
- extra pan
- 3 to 4 beakers
- dry dye for selected colors
- CA crystals
- Synthrapol
- Bluette™ gloves
- Salt (optional)

Start:

- Fill the dye pan two-thirds full with water and simmer without boiling.
- Mix 3 to 4 colors in separate beakers.
- Dissolve the dry dye powder
- Add 1/2 teaspoon CA crystals and 1/2 cup boiling water to each beaker.
- Add 1 tablespoon of CA crystals to the dye pan, as colors need to grab into the wool quickly.
- Squeeze the excess water from the wool, but not too dry.
- By picking up the middle of the wool swatch, place the edges of the wool into the basket first. Do the same for all swatches, if you have more than one.
- Add the first color to the dye pan and then place the basket into the dye pan. If the wool floats up, gently press it down with a gloved hand.
- Once the water clears, remove the basket and place it in the empty pan, then add the next color to the dye pan.

Kettle Spotdye Technique: One-quarter yard natural wool. Colors used: [135, 1/8], [130, 1/16], [366, 1/16] in separate beakers. This technique is like cooking pasta with a strainer. The basket pattern is transferred to the wool, leaving added texture...extra fun.

- With a gloved hand, pick up the wool edges and place the center of the swatch into the basket. This allows the color to grab into the wool at different locations.

- Repeat the steps until you are happy and the entire wool swatch is dyed.

- When the dye pan water is clear, remove the wool from the basket and place it into the dye pan to simmer, without boiling, for one hour.

- Wash with detergent, rinse well, and dry.

1. Kettle Spot Dye Technique: 3 colors in separate beakers with 1 teaspoon CA crystals dissolved in each, dye pan with hot water, and 1 teaspoon CA crystals dissolved. Two quarter yards pre-soaked wool.

2. Pick the wool up in the middle of the swatch, and place the ends into the basket. Use a glove (shown here without a glove for clarity). First add the lightest or brightest color to the pan.

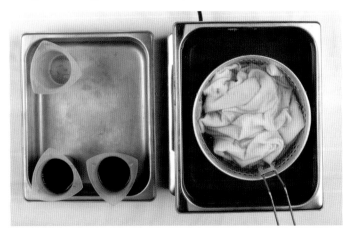

3. With the first color in the dye pan, lower the basket into the dye pan. A slight press, with a gloved hand may be needed at first to keep the wool in the water.

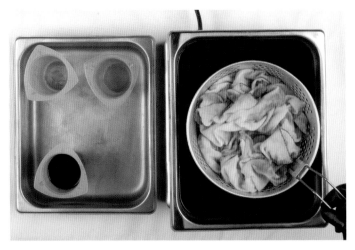

4. The basket is removed from the dye pan once the water clears of color. The wool is removed from the basket. Flip the wool over so the raw edges of the wool are now on top and replace the wool in the basket.

5. The second color is added to the dye pan, and the basket is lowered into the dye pan. The highlights and lowlights are already visible in the wool.

6. The wool is flipped again while the third color is in the dye pan. The wool is flipped to avoid any undyed areas and create a great deal of interest in each wool swatch.

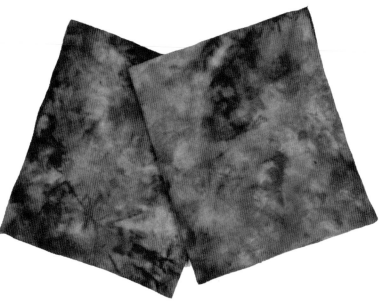

7. Once the water clears of dye, the wool may be placed into the dye pan to simmer, without boiling, for one hour. Wash with detergent, rinse well and dry.

Kettle Spot Dye results. The basket is fun for a quick Spotdye. It provides a variety of value changes as well as intensities. The patterns left on the wool are such a bonus. This is one of my favorite techniques due to its simplicity and the results.

Kettle Spot Dye: The purple, greens and yellows remain visible due to the technique and the citric acid crystals. Notice the basket pattern in the far right corner.

Kettle Spot Dye Technique: This example has incredible value changes and shows, in the middle, the basket pattern transferred onto the wool. What great fall foliage.

NATURAL SPOTDYE TECHNIQUE

There never seems to be enough light wool for projects. This technique speaks to that issue. Sometimes, just a hint of color is needed without having stark white. I find that even though I try to use the smallest amount of dye it may be too much. This technique is very much like the Northern Spot Dye without all the color. The goal is to have as little color as possible added to white or natural wool.

Gather:

- wool, 2 quarter yard swatches or desired amount, pre-soaked 30 minutes.
- 2-inch half hotel dye pan
- 2 beakers
- dry dye for selected colors
- CA crystals
- Synthrapol
- Bluette™ gloves
- Salt (optional)

Spotted Natural Technique: This technique is meant to offer very little color change in the original wool. This technique meets the need for those necessary very light neutral wool colors in projects without being stark white.

Spotted Natural Technique: one-quarter yard white wool. The weakest color solutions possible are used in this technique. Leftover color used: Chocolate Brown [502] and Poppy Red [340] (1 toothpick). Very little dye attaches to a toothpick when dissolved.

Start:

- Gather leftover dye bath or make a new color. The desired concentration of color is so very weak, like dirty dishwater, that it is barely there. Any pale color will do fine.
- Place your dye pan on the counter top.
- Squeeze the water from the wool until it feels paper dry.
- Arrange the wool in the pan by draping it first so that the wool is open.
- Start in the middle of the pan and use your fingertips to bring the wool into the pan, while creating hills and valleys. The tighter the wool fits into the dye pan, the better.
- Add the first color randomly, a little at a time.
- With your gloved hand, make a fist, hold your arm straight, put your fist on the wool, and lean into your fist. This is the easiest way to disperse the dye without fatiguing your body.
- Add the second color and continue the pour–press technique.
- Overlap your colors a bit; there will be some undyed areas in this technique.
- When finished adding dye, look between the hills and valleys and add color accordingly, still pressing as you go.
- Dissolve 1 tablespoon of CA crystals into 1 cup boiling water and place under each corner of the wool.
- Cover and simmer, without boiling, for one hour.
- Wash with detergent, rinse well, and dry.

2. With the dye pan on the counter, pour the first color onto the wool randomly. The gloved hand is pressing onto the wool to disperse the color. This is the same pressing that is used in the Northern Spot Dye Technique. Note, again, how weak the color is for the success of this technique.

3. Pressing continues as the second color is randomly poured onto the wool.

1. Spotted Natural Technique: pre-soaked wool, 2 very weak colors in separate beakers with CA crystals dissolved in each. Aluminum foil is optional. When the pan is too large a foil bridge may be made to compact the wool, as seen here. The wool is drawn into the pan with hills and valleys, as in the Northern and Southern Spotdye Technique.

4. Add dissolved CA crystals in water under the corners of the wool to prevent burnt wool. Simmer the wool, without boiling, for one hour, adding water as necessary.

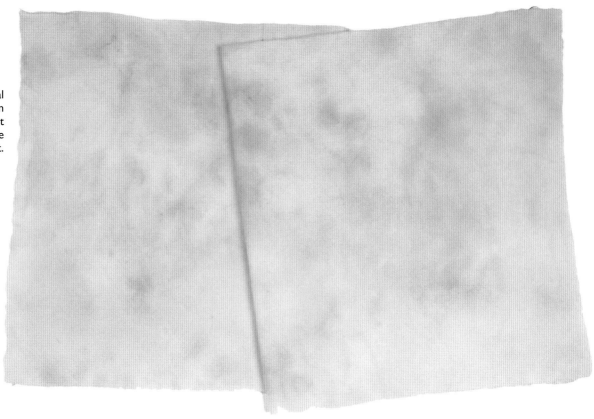

This Spotted Natural wool is a little darker in value than preferred, but it will find a welcome place in a future project.

Spotted Naturals Technique: One-quarter yard, natural wool, using very little leftover colors, Acid Yellow [135] and Chocolate Brown [502] (1 toothpick), dissolved in boiling water. The weak color adds needed dimension to the wool.

The Spotted Natural Technique will transform ordinary white and
natural wool with a flat appearance to a very light value with lowlights.

This group of wool represents the
Northern and Southern Spotdye, Dip Dye
and Spotted Natural Techniques, balancing
warm, and cool colors in different values.

IT'S A YELLOW DAY!

LINGERING SUNSHINE!

I use Sun Yellow [119], for my true primary yellow. Yellow is closer to the top of the value scale than the other colors. It is the color to leave the dye pan last. It will take more yellow dry dye powder to change a color than any of the others.

Experiment with a yellow day, and make the secondary colors orange and green. By using more yellow with very little blue dry dye powder, the result is yellow-green. Increase your amount of blue and watch the color move to a blue-green. Have fun and play.

DIP DYE TECHNIQUE

The goal of this technique is to have one color in a light, medium, and dark value on a single wool swatch without horizontal lines. I consider this a classic technique.

Sometime you may see people standing on chairs holding coat hangers with wool attached. There are all kinds of clever maneuvers to eliminate arm fatigue, while holding the wool over very deep dye pots. With the shallow dye pans, it is easier to stand on the floor and use your arm.

I recommend the wool be held in the strong arm from start to finish. The motion of the working arm is up and down without stopping. It is the constant motion that prevents the horizontal lines between values.

If you are dyeing this technique for a motif, there is a general guide for length and width. Depending on the height of your rug hooking, it is 4 to 5 times the length and 1-1/2 to 2 times the width of the motif.

Gather:

- wool, 2 quarter yard swatches or desired amount, pre-soaked 30 minutes
- 4-inch half hotel dye pan
- beaker
- dry dye powder
- CA crystals
- Synthrapol
- Bluettes™ gloves
- Salt (optional)

Dip Dye Technique: Natural, celery, and oatmeal wools. Dyed together, this cool color combination provides a more distinct variation by starting with different wools.

Dip Dye Technique: one-quarter yard natural wool. Colors used: Acid Golden Yellow [199, 1/2] + [119, 1/8] + [135, 1/2], in one beaker. Traditionally, dip dyed wool will have a relative light, medium, and dark value in one swatch.

Beginning with a light textured wool, a Dip Dye Technique holds true to light, medium, and dark values in one swatch. The dye bath strength is relative to the starting wool. *Wool donated by Pat Cross.*

Start:

- Fill the dye pan two-thirds full of water and 1 tablespoon CA crystals and simmer without boiling.

- Make one color; it is easier to make a stronger dye solution and use what is needed.

- Add the color to the dye pan, adjusting the amount as needed.

- Squeeze the excess water from the swatches.

- With your glove on, gather the ends of the wool length in one hand. Once you begin dipping it is better to leave the swatches in that hand.

- Begin the dipping process. About one-third of the wool is lowered into the dye pan as you dip constantly. This will be your dark value.

- Continue this up-and-down motion and then dip the middle third into the pan which will become your medium value. Keep an eye on the amount of dye in the pan while moving the wool up and down; you will need to have enough color to be in the pan for your lightest value.

- The last third is the lightest value. For the last value, the tips are dipped into the pan by opening your hand into the color, and allow the dye into the tips.

- Squeeze out the excess water, then continue to dip until the color in the pan is very weak.

- Lay or fold the values in the pan so that they are immersed and spaced apart, dark value away from light value.

- Simmer, without boiling, for one hour.

- Wash with detergent, rinse well, and dry.

1. Dip Dye Technique: pre-soaked wool, one color, dye pan with water and dissolved CA crystals brought to a simmer without boiling.

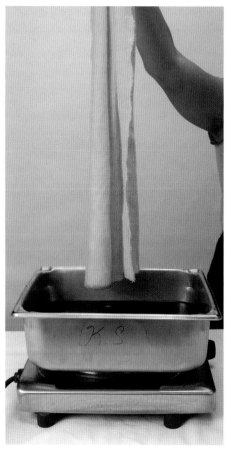

2. With color in the dye pan, the gloved hand will hold the wool at one end. It is better to start and end with the wool in the same hand; it prevents distortion of the values.

3. Begin dipping the first third of the wool swatch up and down, to establish the dark value in the wool swatch.

4. As the dipping up and down continues, the medium value is established by lowering the middle third of the swatch into the dye pan.

A single wool swatch with a light, medium, and dark value is the desired goal. The value change is always relative to the chosen color and the wool that is used.

5. The last value is created by opening your hand to allow color onto the last third of the swatch. Maintain a keen eye on the amount of dye in the pan prior to dipping the tips into the pan.

6. The tips are removed immediately after the light value is established. The gloves need to be able to resist boiling water.

7. The eye determines the values and typically the wool is divided into thirds. It may be necessary to have more dark than medium value. This technique allows flexibility in the result.

These two quarter yard wool swatches were dip dyed together, the Glen Plaid is not as satisfying as the solid in value change. This does not prevent the two from being used in the same project with great success.

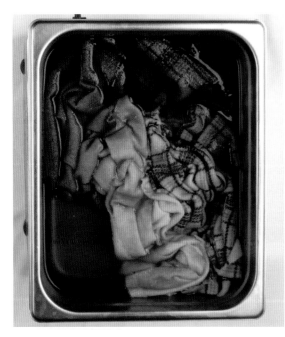

8. When the values are present in the wool and the water is almost clear of dye, the wool may be layered with the light value on top and set according to standards.

Dip Dye Technique: Natural wool. The dark, medium, and light values are relative to this swatch and clearly defined.

It's a YELLOW Day

Dip Dye Technique: One-half yard, natural wool, and dye, Acid Brilliant Violet [817, 1/32], used as needed. Dip Dyed wool is very versatile in projects. They always make great fruit.

Dip Dye Technique: One-half yard, sunflower wool. A leftover green color was used as needed. Note the yellow highlights from the sunflower wool used.

DOUBLE DIP DYE TECHNIQUE

In this technique we build on the Single Dip Technique. It starts out the same, but with the addition of a second color we begin to fold the wool. The addition of the second color adds depth, while the folded wool is creased. It is the folds that act as a resist to the second color in the rest of the wool. Have fun with various color combinations.

I recommend the wool be held in the strong arm from start to finish. For the dipping portion, the motion needs to be up and down without stopping. It is the constant motion that prevents the horizontal lines between values. There is a general guide for length and width if you are dyeing this technique for a motif. Depending on the height of your rug hooking, the swatch is 4 to 5 times the length and 1-1/2 to 2 times the width of the motif.

Gather:

- wool, 2 quarter yard swatches or desired amount, pre-soaked 30 minutes
- 4-inch half hotel dye pan
- 2 beakers
- dry dye powder
- 2 colors
- CA crystals
- Synthrapol
- Bluettes™ gloves
- salt (optional)

Start:

- Fill the dye pan two-thirds full of water and 1 tablespoon CA crystals; simmer without boiling.
- Make 2 colors; the second color should enhance the first.
- Add the first color to the dye pan, adjusting the amount as needed.
- Squeeze the excess water from the swatches.
- With your glove on, gather the ends of the length of the wool in one hand. Once you begin dipping it is better to leave the swatches in that hand
- Begin the dipping process up and down, about one-third of the wool length. This will be your dark value.
- Continue this up and down motion as you lower the middle third into the pan. This becomes your

Dip Dye Technique: Natural, oatmeal and grey wool dyed together. The oatmeal wool, center, is less intense due to added texture and the starting color of the wool. Another great reason to mix the starting wools.

Double Dip Dye Technique: Celery, natural, and sunflower wool dyed together. Notice that the orange background flowers are the direct complement of blue, making a very harmonious picture.

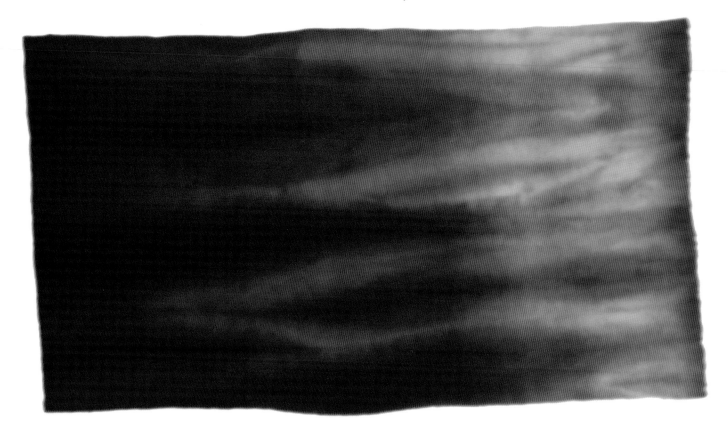

Try to avoid horizontal lines between values in any Dip Dye. A continuous up and down motion of the wool prevents this.

medium value. Keep an eye on the amount of dye in the pan while moving the wool up and down; you need to have enough color for your lightest value.

• The last third of the wool swatch is the lightest value. The tips are dipped into the pan as you gently open your hand and allow the dye into the tips.

• Squeeze out the excess water, then continue the dipping until the color is very weak in the pan.

• Lift the entire swatch out of the pan and add the second color.

• Lay the dark end of the wool in one corner of pan, then fold the wool back and forth over itself, maintaining the values created by the dip. This again is constant movement, although now we are folding the wool instead of dipping.

• Lift the wool up and move the ends to the opposite corner of the pan, then fold the wool back and forth. Once this step begins, it is best if the wool stays in the same hand. Remember, it is the opposite side of the pan, not the opposite end of the wool. The lightest value is in your hand.

• Continue this folding motion until the water is almost clear. This is the time to place the ends in your hand, the lightest value, into the water to pick up a little color.

• When the desired color combinations have been achieved, lay or fold the wool so that it is immersed into the water, keeping the darkest and lightest values apart.

• Simmer, without boiling, for one hour.

• Wash with detergent, rinse well, and dry.

1. Double Dip Dye Technique: pre-soaked wool, two colors in separate beakers, dye pan with water, and CA crystals dissolved while heating. The first color is in the pan.

2. The fist step is to complete a dip dye, with the light, medium and dark values established. The wool is then lifted out of the water.

4. The wool is lifted out of the water, and moved to the opposite corner and folded back toward the center of the pan. Continue this folding method until very little color remains in the pan.

3. The second color is added to the dye pan, and the folding begins. The darkest value of the wool swatch is placed in one corner, and the wool is folded over itself. The lightest value remains out of the water for now.

5. When very little color remains in the dye pan, the tips go into the water. The wool is gently stacked and simmers, without boiling, for one hour. The wool is then washed with detergent, rinsed, and dried.

It is the addition of the second color and the folds which create more depth in the wool swatch. This adds amazing interest to the traditional dip dye technique.

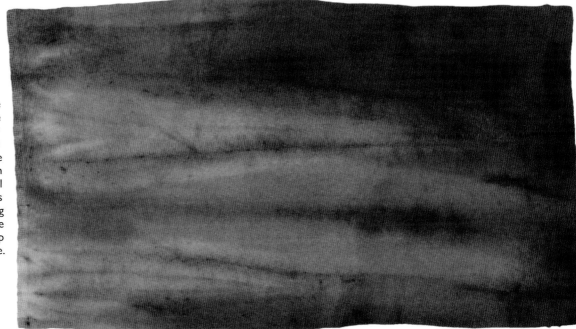

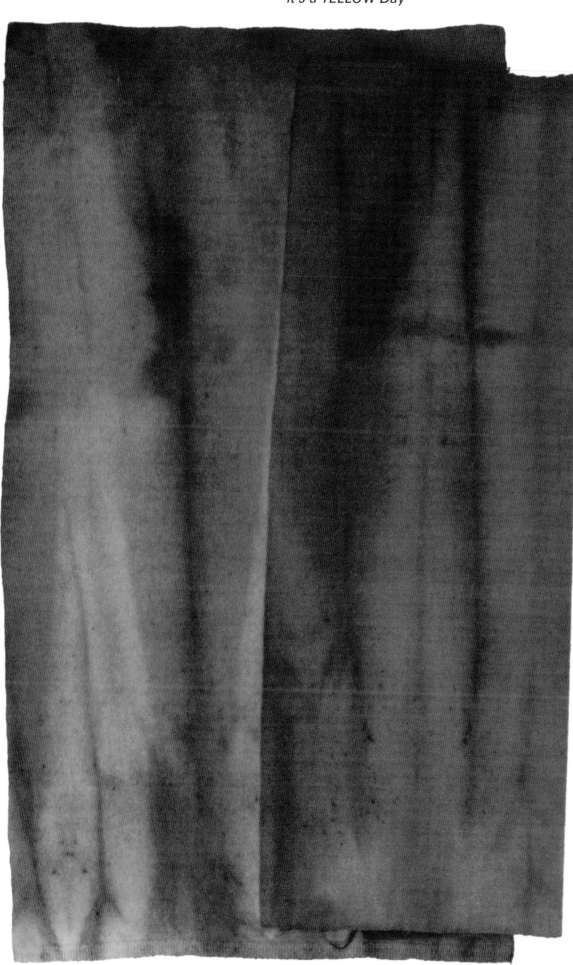

Double Dip Technique results. The second color is a much darker value than the first color to add another magical element to the wool. This shows oatmeal wool, right, and natural, left.

It's a YELLOW Day

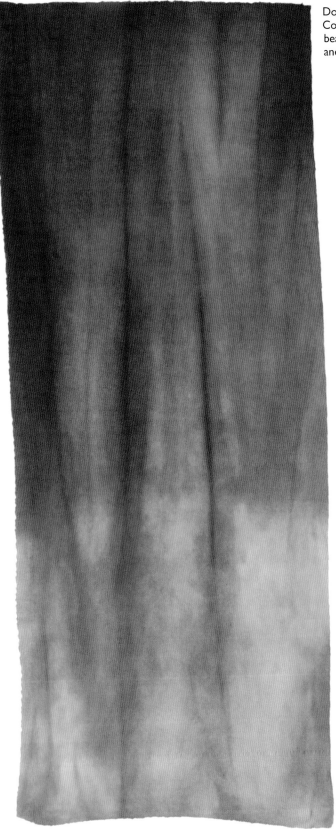

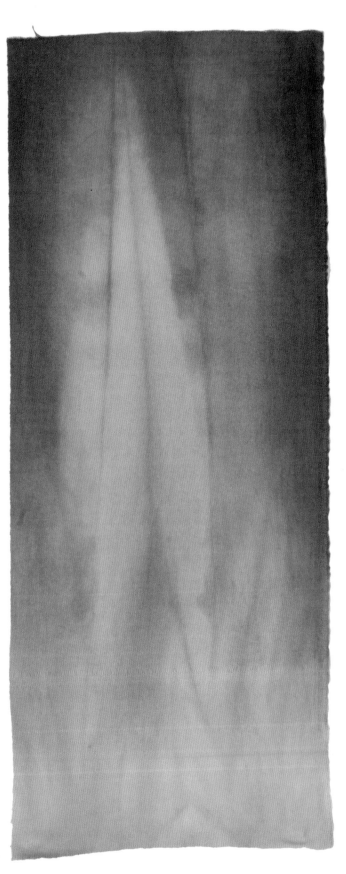

Double Dip Technique: One-quarter yard of celery wool. Colors used: [233, 1/8] and Black [672, 1/32], in separate beakers, as needed. The horizontal line was not a goal here and is a result of the wool not moving in a fluid motion.

Double Dip Technique: One-quarter yard of celery wool. The second and darker color green adds definition to the folds in the wool. To me, it is much more exciting this way.

"Heather's Graduation," a high school graduation gift designed and hooked by me for my niece, Heather Trautman Burroughs. The wool used for the eagle was from the Double Dip & Twist Techniques. *Courtesy of Heather Trautman Burroughs, Greenwood, South Carolina.*

DOUBLE DIP & TWIST TECHNIQUE

This technique builds on both the Single and Double Dip Techniques for applying color onto the wool. The dip starts this technique, then twisting replaces the folding of the double dip. There are two colors used in this technique that complement each other, the second one darker than the first. When dry, the dyed wool swatch is torn across the fold and used light to dark.

Again, I recommend the wool be held in the strong arm from start to finish. The movement is a continuous up and down motion for the dipping portion. It is the constant motion that prevents the horizontal lines between values.

If you are dyeing this technique for a motif, there is a general guide for length and width. Based on the height of your rug hooking, the swatch should be 4 to 5 times the length and 1-1/2 to 2 times the width of the motif.

Gather:

- wool, 2 quarter yard swatches or desired amount, pre-soaked 30 minutes
- 4-inch half hotel dye pan
- 2 beakers
- dry dye powder
- 2 colors
- CA crystals
- Synthrapol
- Bluettes™ gloves
- salt (optional)

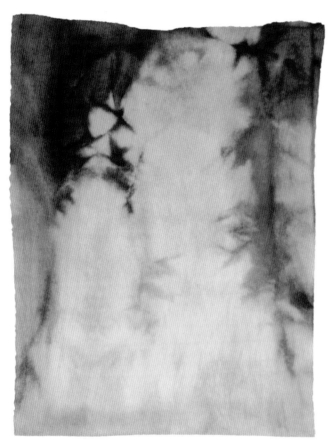

Double Dip & Twist Technique, this wool cut in half is ready to be used. This is one-half of the swatch containing a light to dark value. The strips would be cut lengthwise for traditional rug hooking.

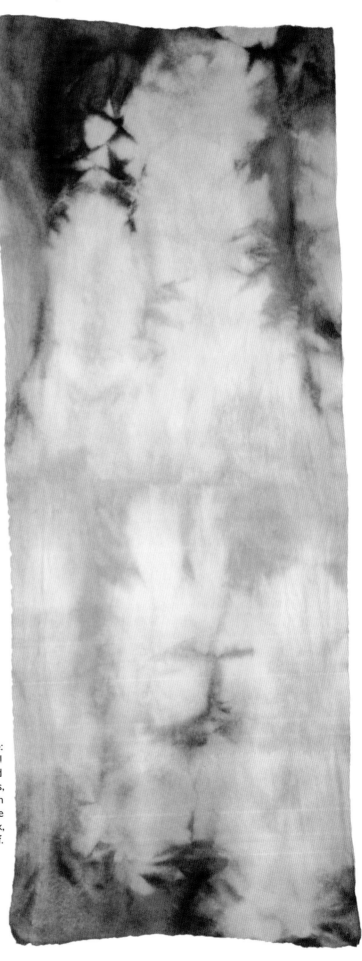

Double Dip & Twist Technique: One-quarter yard of natural wool. Colors used: [119, 1/8] and [502, 1/32], in separate beakers, as needed. The wool is folded in half to start this technique. The values, light, medium, and dark, are present on each half.

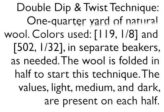

Start:

- Fill the dye pan two-thirds full of water
- Add 1 tablespoon CA crystals and simmer without boiling.
- Make 2 dye baths; the second color should enhance the first.
- Add the first color to the dye pan, adjusting the amount as needed.
- Squeeze the excess water from the swatches.
- Fold the swatch in half lengthwise, thereby shortening the swatch.
- Gather the folded edge of the swatch.
- With your gloved hand, hold the wool firmly and begin dipping the ends of the wool into the pan. Like the dip dye, value is created by lowering the wool by thirds into the dye pan. Continue the dipping while lowering the wool into the pan, until the water is clear.
- Lift the wool out of the pan and add the second color.
- As the wool re-enters the pan, begin twisting the swatches as you press into the pan. Repeat if desired.
- When there is only a little color in the pan, twist, and leave to simmer, without boiling, for one hour.
- Wash with detergent, rinse well, and dry.
- Tear the swatches down the fold, creating two swatches in light to dark values.

1. The wool swatch is folded in half lengthwise and picked up by the fold.

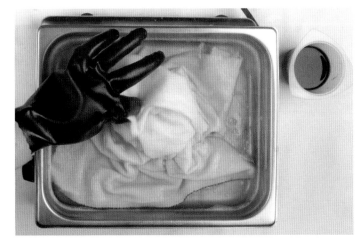

2. Dip Dye & Twist Technique uses 2 colors with 1 teaspoon CA crystals dissolved in each beaker, a dye pan with water and one teaspoon dissolved CA crystals, and pre-soaked wool swatch. The first color is in the pan.

3. After the values, light, medium, and dark are established, the second color is ready to be added in preparation for the twisting.

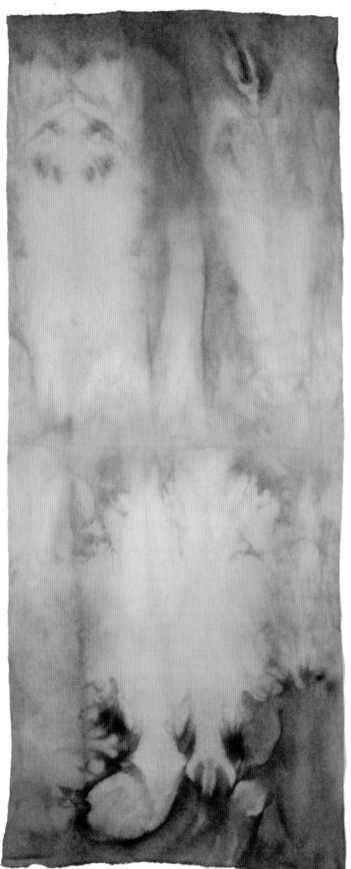

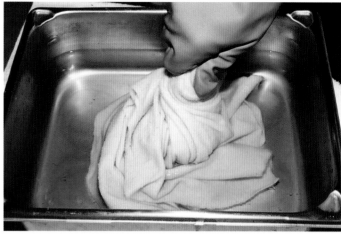

4. This demonstrates how the wool is twisted as it is being pressed into the dye pan once the values have been established.

5. Twist the wool as it is pressed into the pan. The wool is then lifted from the pan and twisted again. This step is repeated until you are satisfied with the color.

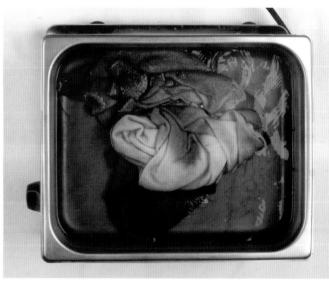

Double Dip & Twist Technique: One-quarter yard, celery wool, using 2 colors, first [119, 1/8] + [440, 1/128], then add [502, 1/32] as needed. The brown appears to be moving like a wave over the green color.

6. The wool is simmered while it is twisted, the lighter tips stay on the top until the water is clear of dye. Simmer, without boiling, for one hour. Wash with detergent, rinse well, and dry.

Although this result is darker, the light, medium, and dark values are accounted for. The uses for this dyed wool are endless. It could easily be used in traditional rug hooking or a penny rug.

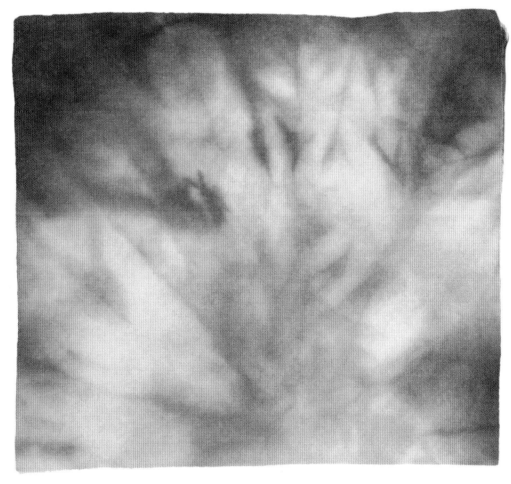

When folded each side shows how much movement is created as a result of the twisting after the double dip. Color combinations are endless.

WHY NOT ORANGE?

recommend you try mixing your reds and yellows to create orange. Once you have mastered the range of yellow-orange to orange-red, try Bright Orange [233], a true secondary color. Orange is below yellow on the value scale, which indicates that it takes more orange color than red or blue to change a color.

I love orange, probably because of the fall colors and pumpkins, not to mention my Halloween birthday. As the direct complement of blue, the combinations are endless. Orange and blue-green together are so calming. Again, play with mixing colors that contain orange and have fun. You have developed the skills to create the secondary colors as we move through the techniques.

COLOR TRANSITION TECHNIQUE

The goal in this technique is to transition through different colors on one piece of wool. The wool swatch is dyed in thirds, but, as the colors change, there may or may not be a value difference. The change in value depends on the strength of the chosen color.

This technique is fine for small to very large pieces of wool. I have personally dyed from quarter yards up to one yard of wool at a time. With the right size pan and imagination, beautiful sunsets may be dyed using several colors. This is another technique that is great to borrow from Mother Nature, with her incredible blending of colors on display for us to use.

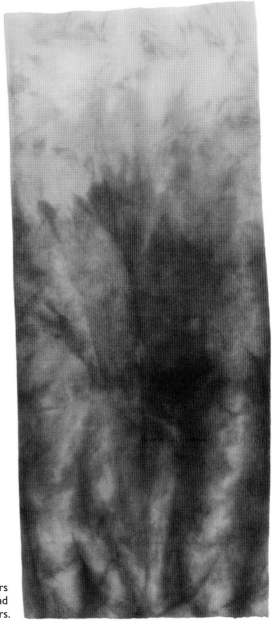

Color Transition Technique: One-quarter yard of celery wool. Colors used: [119, 1/16] + [502, 1/128], [135, 1/32] + Brick [255, 1/128], and [817, 1/32], in separate beakers. This is perfect for garden flowers.

This is my adaptation of "Starry Night" by Vincent Van Gogh. The dyed wool strip on the left shows how the Color Transition Technique was used for most of the rug. This simplified my hooking while mimicking paint strokes that appear cohesive. *Courtesy of Adale, and Terry Woodruff, Newland, NC.*

Gather:

- wool, 2 quarter yard swatches or desired amount, pre-soaked 30 minutes
- 2-inch half hotel dye pan,
- 3 beakers
- dry dye for selected colors
- CA crystals
- Synthrapol
- Bluettes™ gloves
- Salt (optional)

Start:

- Fill the dye pan one-third full.
- Add 1 tablespoon CA crystals.
- Simmer without boiling.
- Mix your colors in three separate beakers.
- Add 1 teaspoon CA crystals to each dye bath and dissolve with 2/3 cup boiling water.
- Place your colors within arm's reach of your dye pan.
- Squeeze excess water from the wool swatches.
- With a gloved hand (I am right-handed so I glove my left hand to hold wool as the right hand is the busy one) hold the ends in your palm. This technique moves quickly.
- Place the first color into the pan and lower one-third of the wool into the pan.
- Spread the wool so the color is absorbed.
- Move the wool around to prevent any undyed areas.

1. Color Transition Technique: 3 colors in separate small beakers, a shallow dye pan with 1/2 inch water heated, 1 teaspoon CA crystals dissolved in the dye pan and in the beakers, and pre-soaked wool. The first color is heating in the pan.

Why Not ORANGE?

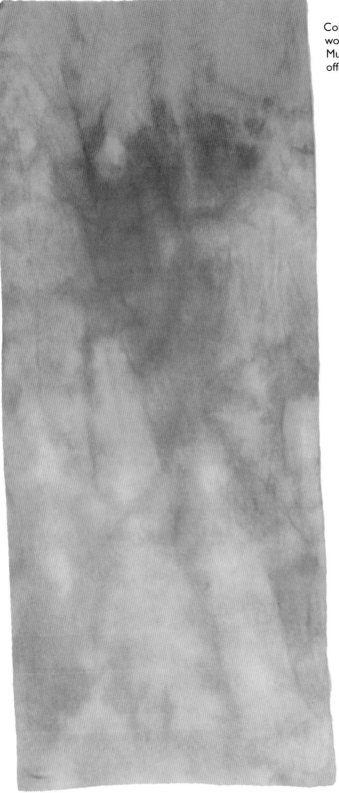

Color Transition Technique: One-quarter yard of white wool. Colors used: Magenta [338], [490+119] and Mustard [122], in separate beakers. This technique offers three different colors on one wool swatch.

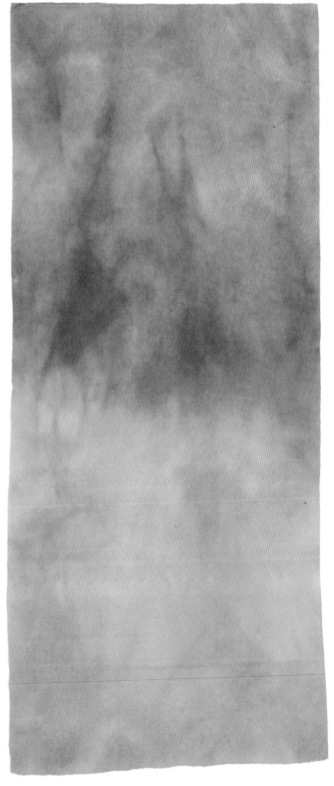

The amount of dry dye used in each color plays a vital role in this technique. If one of the three is a very weak solution it may become lost. This swatch would make a beautiful sunflower nonetheless.

2. With a gloved hand holding one end of the wool, lower the bottom third of the wool and spread it out into the pan to take up the first color.

3. Move the wool to the far end of the pan and add the second color behind the wool. The bottom third of the swatch will stay put for the rest of the technique.

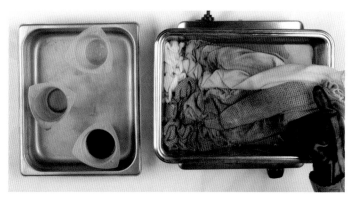

4. Lower the middle third into the pan to take up the color. It is best to spread the wool around in the pan. This technique moves quickly. Keep everything within arms reach.

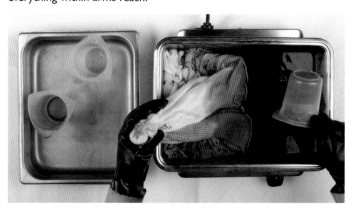

5. With the middle third of the swatch moved to the end of the pan, pour the third and final color behind the wool. The last portion of the wool is placed into the pan to take up the rest of the color.

- Once the water is clear, move the dyed third to the left side of the dye pan (if you are right handed). The wool stays put for the rest of the technique.
- Add the second color behind the swatches being held and lower the next third of the wool into the pan.
- Spread the wool again to absorb the dye and try to avoid moving the resting first third.
- Once the water is cleared, move the middle third of the wool to the left of the pan.
- Add the last color behind the swatch and place the last third of the wool swatch into the pan.
- Move the wool around a little to absorb the color. This technique does not require a large volume of water, but, once the water clears, I fill the pan two-thirds full of water to avoid burning the wool.
- Simmer, without boiling, for one hour.
- Wash with detergent, rinse well, and simmer.

6. Add hot water under the wool to prevent burning the wool. There is such a small amount of water in this technique that it is necessary to add water occasionally. Simmer, without boiling, for one hour. Wash with detergent, rinse well and dry.

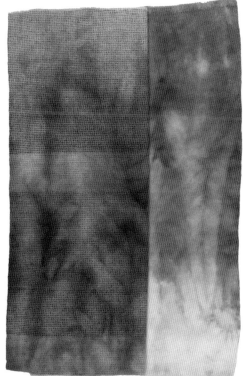

Color Transition Technique: The values, and intensities at the end of the process depend on several conditions. Color selection, the amount of dry dye powder, and the starting liquid all play a role.

Color Transition Technique: One-quarter yard of white wool. Colors are [490 + 119], Violet, [818], and Turquoise, [478], in separate beakers. This could be an ocean floor, cut horizontally.

This example is a yard of wool folded into a quarter yard. This technique may be used to dye larger amounts for a sky, or for ground cover. The transition of one color to the next makes this technique exciting.

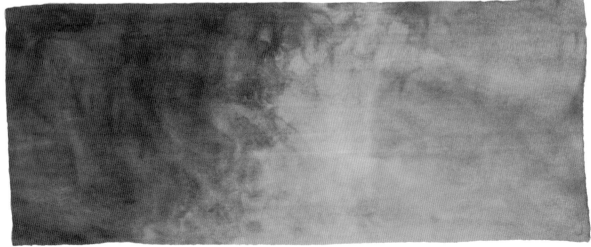

This was a yard of wool, but one-half yard remains. It is now being used in a sunflower pattern. Wools dyed in this technique may be cut vertical or horizontal.

The same yard of wool cut or torn horizontal with the length and traditionally hand hooked. For this effect, the strips need to remain in order as the wool is cut. It is always exciting how it is going to look.

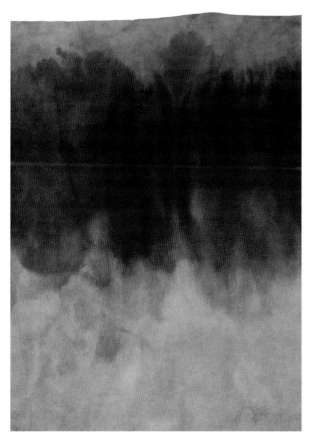

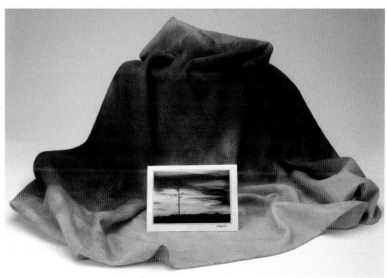

Color Transition Technique: One yard of natural wool. Inspiration may be found anywhere, and for this sky I was inspired by photographer, Harley Bonham's, "Arizona Sunset." With Harley's permission I am able to show you nature is our color teacher if we look. *Courtesy of Harley Bonham, Phoenix, Arizona.*

Color Transition Technique: One yard natural wool. When dyeing yardage, a larger pan is needed and more water. It is best to have all of the colors within arms reach. The colors used are [117], [233], [351], [817], [487], and [672], in varied amounts. Dye by eye!

111

Jar Dye Technique: Natural wool swatches with 2 colors: [351, 1/16] and [255, 1/32] in separate beakers. The first color goes into a Pyrex measuring cup. The mottling is a result of dipping infrequently.

JAR DYE TECHNIQUE

When I think of all the ways to dye wool, this is another that I consider somewhat classical. Canning jars become vessels for us to add color to wool, creating balanced values from light to dark. The wool swatches are much smaller, so they can fit inside the jar.

This technique, in my opinion is higher maintenance. Traditionally one color is used, but I prefer to add a second color to my jars. I limit my jars to 6 because they fit inside my pan. More jars could be used, so find what makes you comfortable.

To become McGown-certified in the mid-1990s, Becky Trent and I used novelty dyeing for our student projects. It consisted of 12 jars and swatches. You can imagine 2 colors and a great deal of crossing the colors back and forth over the 12 jars. It was a great challenge and fun for us.

Gather:

- wool, a quarter yard divided into 6 swatches, pre-soaked 30 minutes

- 4-inch half hotel dye pan

1. Jar Dye Technique: pre-soaked wool swatches, wide mouth (quart) canning jars, dye pan, 1 or 2 colors, CA crystals, and salt. If using 2 colors the first color is made in a 1 cup Pyrex measuring cup. The jars are placed into the empty dye pan.

- 6 one-quart, wide mouth canning jars
- dry dye
- 1 cup Pyrex measuring glass
- CA crystals
- Synthrapol
- Salt (optional)

Start:

- In your 1 cup Pyrex measuring glass, make your color, adding 1 cup of boiling water to dissolve dry dye.

- Place your empty dye pan on the counter and place the empty canning jars in the pan.

- Into the first jar, pour off exactly 1/2 cup of the color.

- Refill the Pyrex cup with tap water to the 1 cup level and stir. It is important to keep some order to your jars with respect to dark to light values. You have just poured your darkest value.

- Into the next jar, pour off 1/2 cup of the new dye bath.

- Refill the Pyrex cup with tap water to the 1 cup level and stir.

- Continue this procedure until all the jars contain 1/2 cup of dye. There will be 1/2 cup unused color left in your Pyrex cup, so pour it down the drain.

- Return to the first jar and fill it with hot tap water up to an inch below the neck of the jar, leaving enough room for the wool.

- Add 1/2 teaspoon of salt and 1/2 teaspoon of CA crystals to each jar and stir well.

- Squeeze the excess water from the wool swatches.

- Using the tongs, hold one end of the swatch and start dipping the swatch up and down. Begin with the lightest value and leave the swatch immersed in the jar. This eliminates any contamination of the dark value color to the lighter values.

- In the same way, dip a swatch in each jar until all the jars contain wool. Traditional jar dyeing results in a very smooth color distribution in the swatch. This occurs by dipping approximately 20 to 40 times, every 10 to 15 minutes. How many times and how frequently you dip are personal choices. A mottled appearance occurs by dipping fewer times and less frequently.

Jar Dye Technique: One-quarter yard, natural wool swatches with 2 colors: [119, 1/16] + [130, 1/128] and [199, 1/16] + [502, 1/128] in separate beakers. The first color goes into the Pyrex measuring cup. This is the easiest way possible to value dye consistently in 6 to 8 swatches.

- Fill your pan with 2 inches of water and place the pan on stove top, covered with foil. Set a timer for the desired 10 to 15 minutes and simmer without boiling. When the timer rings, remove the foil and repeat the dipping; this continues for one hour, dipping every 10 to 15 minutes.

- Remove the pan from the stove. There may be some color left in the jar.

- Empty the darkest value first, running the swatch under water and setting it aside until all the jars are empty. Starting with the darkest value prevents contamination of the lighter values.

- Wash the swatches with detergent, rinse well, and dry.

When I add a second color, I do so by eye. I enjoy the dimensions created in the wool by adding the second color.

4. Refill the Pyrex cup with tap water to the one cup level and stir.

2. The selected color is made in the Pyrex cup and filled to the one cup mark. Half cup is poured into the first jar and will become the darkest value. Add tap water to the Pyrex cup bringing the water level back to the 1 cup measure and stir. Note: The jars are set on the counter for clarity.

5. Pour one-half cup color into the next jar. Notice the value changing as you pour off dye. The first three jars are your darkest values.

3. Pour one-half cup color into the next jar.

6. Refill the Pyrex cup to the one cup level with tap water and stir.

7. Continue this method of pouring one-half cup color into each jar, until all of the jars contain one-half cup color. **The last jar only receives one-half cup color.**

9. With each jar containing one-half cup color, increase the water level in each jar using tap water. Leave an inch or more at the top to make room for the wool. Begin dipping the individual swatch into the color. Salt is optional at this time, one-half teaspoon per jar.

8. The Pyrex cup will contain one-half cup color when the last jar has color. This leftover half cup is not used. If added to any jar the value results will be distorted.

10. Dip a swatch up and down in the jar and then leave it immersed into the color. When dealing with darker colors start dipping at the lightest value to prevent cross contamination of the darker value color on the lighter values. Each swatch is dipped up and down 20-30 times and the dipping is repeated every 10-15 minutes.

11. Add approximately 2 inches of water to the pan prior to the heat.

13. The foil is removed and the dipping is repeated in each jar.

12. Cover the jars much like in canning food, and set the timer to ring in 15 minutes. More frequent dipping and/or how long you dip determines the absorption rate and location of color on each swatch. If using a second color, I dye by eye to add to each jar.

14. Add one tablespoon CA crystals to a beaker of water and add to each jar as you continue to dip. The one hour time setting begins when the CA crystals go into each jar. Cover with foil and set the timer for 15 minutes, when you will dip again. This continues for one hour. Wash with detergent, rinse well and dry.

Jar dye Technique: One-quarter yard, celery wool swatches used with Plum [822,1/16]. The celery wool brings warmth to the cool purple color, a great combination. Notice each swatch has two or three values in it. Yummy!

Jar Dye Technique: Natural wool swatches. The green color is a combination of [490 + 119] and the direct complement of red. The intensity of pure color in each of these swatches encourages the values to dance around the basket in harmony.

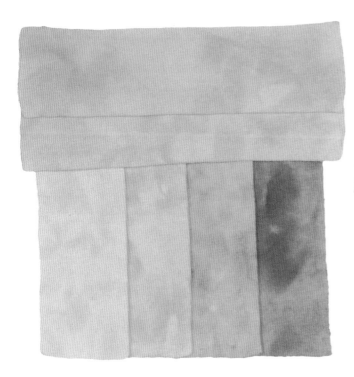

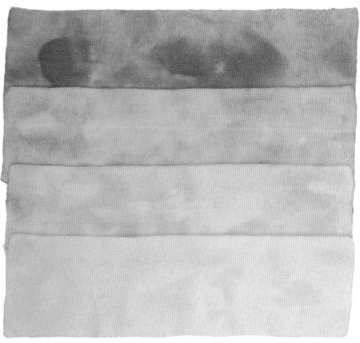

Two of the six values dyed appear too close in value. The bottom four are ideal, an they will be used. This is such a great yellow green.

The contrasting highlights and lowlights indicate reduced and infrequent dipping, which is my desired goal. The balance in the value change shows from one swatch to the next, and this is the reward.

Jar Dye Technique: One-quarter yard natural wool using leftover colors blue green and purple mud. Mud is created by all of the leftover color poured into one jar with a lid. The mud will take on different colors at different times.

FLOATING DYE TECHNIQUE

This technique gives you the opportunity for snow storms, pale colors, and a sunny days... anything is possible. I witnessed this dye technique at Marion Ham's Quail Hill Workshop, for my very first rug. The procedure did not have a name and, at the time, I did not have a clue. I watched as Tom dyed my background, one swatch at a time. When the swatches are used, they are cut, mixed together, and used randomly.

Floating the dye onto the wool provides a great deal of control when applying color in lighter values. The fun is in the color and how it is placed on the wool, which is great to see in a rug. Another Quail Hill Design received a snow storm from this technique, as Santa carried his tree through the blizzard.

Gather:

- wool, a quarter yard divided into 4 or more swatches, pre-soaked 30 minutes.
- 4-inch half hotel dye pan
- stew pan
- beaker
- dry dye powder
- teaspoon measure
- CA crystals
- Synthrapol
- salt (optional)
- Bluettes™ gloves

Start:

- Fill the dye pan and the stew pan two-thirds full with water
- Add 1 tablespoon CA crystals and simmer without boiling.
- Make your color in a beaker.
- Squeeze the excess water from the wool swatches and place aside.
- Place the first swatch into the dye pan, lying flat under the water; it will float. Avoid folding the wool or having too large a piece of wool in the dye pan.
- Spoon the color onto the wool by floating the dye out of the teaspoon. Try to avoid puddles of color on the wool.
- When you have achieved the desired result, place the swatch into the stew pan to simmer.

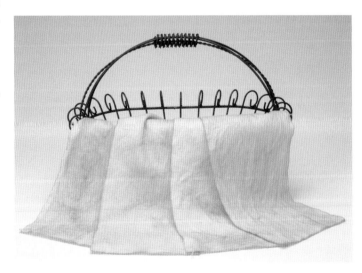

Floating Technique: Natural wool swatches. Colors used: [502, 1/128] + [560, 1/128] in one beaker. These swatches are designed to be cut and mixed together to create movement. They are perfect for landscapes.

118

I share my parents 50th wedding anniversary rug, so that you can see the cloud color. This is the result of floating dye on wool. The wool used was a combination of the Floating and Spotted Natural Dye Techniques. *Courtesy of Frankie & Larry Bushey, Greenwood, South Carolina. Mom now resides in Heaven.*

- The next swatch goes into the dye pan and the same steps repeated.

- Repeat this process until all of the swatches contain color. There will be slight differences in value in the swatches, which is a goal of this technique.

- Place all the swatches in the same pan and simmer, without boiling, for one hour.

- Wash in detergent, rinse well, and dry.

1. Floating Technique: Two pans are used, the dye pan and the stew pan. Both contain 1 tablespoon of CA crystals. The quarter yard of natural wool is cut into swatches to fit the pan. The first swatch is in the pan and the color is spooned randomly onto the water to float onto the wool.

2. Moving slowly and depositing dye in one place will create spots of dark value. This is not my goal, but is shown here for clarity.

3. Avoiding puddles of color takes a little practice. If this occurs use the spoon to quickly move the color around in the pan to disperse the dye onto the wool.

4. When satisfied with the color application, the swatch is moved to the stew pan and the next swatch is placed into the dye pan, where color is randomly floated onto the wool.

5. Once all of the swatches are dyed and placed into the stew pan, simmer, without boiling, for one hour. Wash with detergent, rinse well and dry. This technique is very controlled, and usually produces a light value. The slight variations of color we see in nature is also seen in this technique.

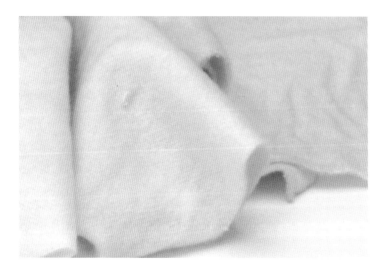

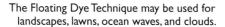

The Floating Dye Technique may be used for landscapes, lawns, ocean waves, and clouds.

Floating Dye Technique: One-quarter yard, natural wool. Colors used: [135, 1/32] + [130, 1/128]. This swatch may be used for faces or skin, with the subtle changes in each swatch.

Floating Dye Technique: One-quarter yard natural wool swatches, torn, and one color: [672, 1/64]. This would be a great stormy sky.

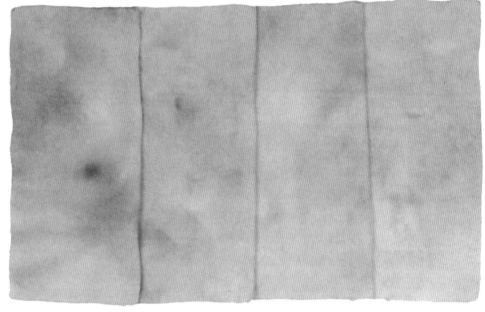

There are so many possibilities to the colors and variations for this technique. The swatches may be used in a variety of ways; a blizzard or background are just a couple of ideas.

NEVER ENOUGH GREEN!

Green is the color with so much range in nature. We see all of the greens right beside each other, from yellow greens to blue greens. On occasion, a variety of greens may be seen in one leaf. Everyone has a favorite color intensity of green. The green color of everything from grasses to oceans may be created in the dye pans. Using the following techniques, it is extra fun to start mixing the primary colors together to find the wide ranges in the color green.

Try your hand at mixing greens and have a green day. On the value scale, green is in the middle, the same as the color red, but it is on the cool side. It takes more green dye powder than blue, but less than orange dry dye powder, to make a color change. Go and have fun.

Note: The next three techniques, painted, paisley, and dry dye, are typically pre-soaked with Synthropal and CA crystals overnight, but definitely for a minimum of 30 minutes.

PAINTED DYE TECHNIQUE

This technique can be used with any design. It allows dyers at all skill levels to paint on wool with sponges, paint brushes, and even spray bottles. Beautiful designs come out of the classroom. Using sponges and brushes, I use this technique to paint skies.

There is no limit to the colors, values, or intensities when painting. Your design fits your need or wants. I have seen designs including trees and flowers, where the painted wool looks as if it had been applied with paints instead of dye. It is definitely time to play here.

A vibrant presentation of color and technique with warm and cool color with highlights and lowlights.

Painted Dye Technique: One-quarter yard natural wool, painted with large paint brushes and several colors. This may be used by cutting vertical or horizontal. There are no limits to the painting technique.

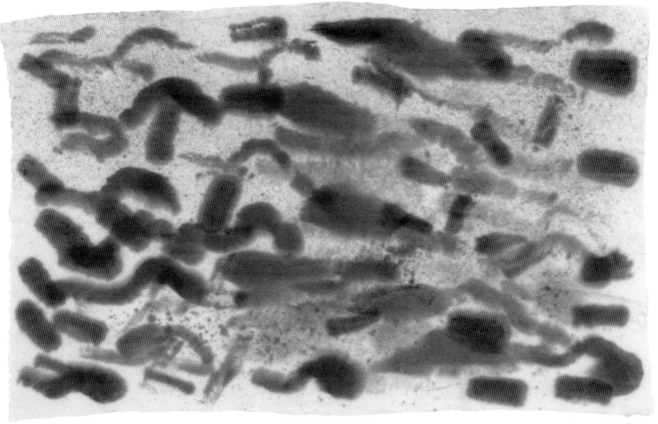

Painted Dye Technique: One-quarter yard, natural wool painted using several colors and paintbrushes.

Painted Dye Technique: One-quarter yard grey wool painted with dissolved dyed from spray bottles. The result is the essence of an impressionist painting in a cool, analogous color relationship.

Gather:

- wool, a quarter yard swatch, pre-soaked in Synthrapol and 1T CA crystals for 30 minutes

- 4-inch half hotel dye pan

- beakers

- dry dye

- a variety of sponges and paint brushes

- spray bottles

- plastic wrap

- aluminum foil

- Bluettes™ gloves

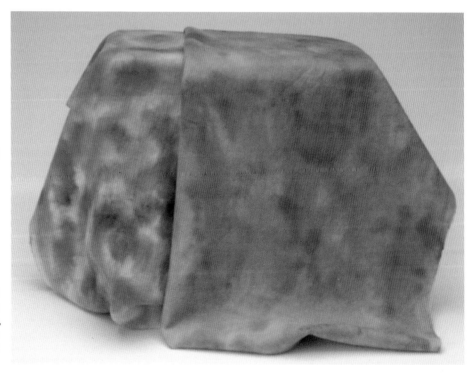

Painted Dye Technique: One-quarter yard sunflower wool, left, and one-quarter yard tan wool on the right. Painting tools may be brushes, squirt or spray bottles, and even sponges. This demonstrates how the colors may expand in the setting process.

1. Painted Dye Technique: wool, pre-soaked Synthrapol and CA crystals overnight, resting on the Glad® Cling Wrap. A variety of colors in separate beakers with 1/2 to1 teaspoon CA crystals dissolved in each beaker, and an assortment of sponges, brushes, and spray bottles that may be used. Aluminum foil and dye pan are used to simmer the wool.

Start:

- Make several colors in separate beakers.
- Add 1/2 teaspoon CA crystals.
- Add boiling water to dissolve crystals and dry dye, stir well.
- Vary the colors both in value and intensity.
- Lay the plastic wrap out on the counter, wider and longer than the size of the wool swatch. You may need to overlap several pieces of the clear wrap.
- Squeeze out excess water (not too dry) and lay the wool flat on top of the plastic wrap.
- Starting with any tool, begin your painting directly on the wool. Paint whatever your imagination leads you; there is no limit to the creativity here.
- When satisfied with your design, roll the bottom edge of the plastic wrap over the bottom edge of the wool and begin rolling the wool, like rolling cookie dough.
- Squeeze the ends together and twist.
- Tear a piece of foil longer than your roll and wrap the rolled wool into the foil, securing the ends.
- Place the roll in the pan and add water until one-third full.
- Cover and simmer, without boiling, for one hour.
- With gloves on, remove the roll from the pan, place it in the sink, and cool with water.
- Carefully remove the foil and cut both ends of the plastic wrap to open. The wool will unravel from the plastic wrap.
- Wash with detergent, rinse well, and dry.

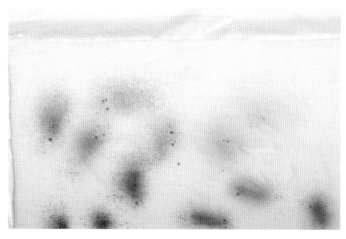

2. After the color is made and cooled, it is poured into spray bottles. The wool swatch is then sprayed with the color. You may decide to spray one or more colors. Painting may be any style or any combination.

125

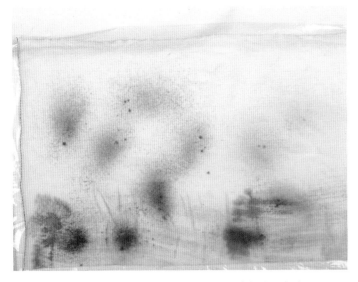

3. This shows how different colors and strokes of the brush show up on the wool. The sprayed color is still visible under the brushstrokes and adds texture and contrast to the wool.

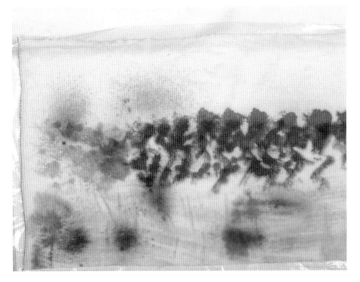

4. Sponge brushes offer a variety of shapes and patterns on the wool.

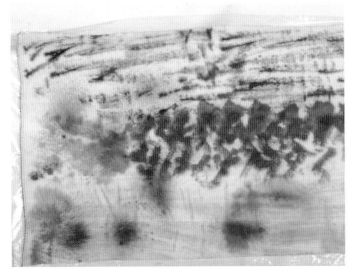

5. Painting the color onto the wool with an artist brush. You may use a variety of brush styles and lengths. Each variety of brush offers a different result.

6. The bottom edge of the plastic wrap is folded over the bottom edge of the wool to start the roll; this protects the painted wool. The entire wool swatch is rolled in the plastic wrap, like cookie dough.

7. The rolled wool is then wrapped in aluminum foil, and ends secured. The roll is placed into the dye pan with water added to the pan. Cover and simmer, without boiling, for one hour. Care must be taken when revealing the surprise; they are very hot. Wash with detergent, rinse well and dry.

Painting may be anything, stripes, trees, sunsets. It is purely a personal choice, so play with different designs. I have seen fascinating designs painted on wool in my dye classes.

Painted Dye Technique: This hooked angel sky was painted with three colors, and a large brush. This worked great for this project. It is a fun technique for many reasons.

Painted Dye Technique: One-quarter yard, white wool painted by several colors in spray bottles.
I enjoy the different applications to the same technique; no two paintings are the same.

Painted Dye Technique: One-quarter yard natural wool is sponged and brushed in a variety of colors.

Painted Dye Technique: Oatmeal wool sponged with a variety of colors. Notice the medium value and color intensity due to the starting value of the oatmeal wool.

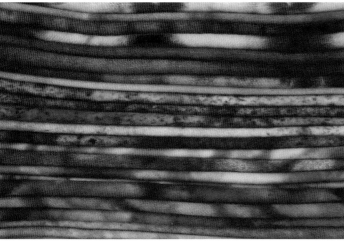

This stack of wool displays the Painted, Paisley and Floating Dry Dye Techniques. Notice the small bits of color popping from the swatches like a candy store of color.

PAISLEY DYE TECHNIQUE

If you have dyed your way from the beginning to this chapter, wow! Look how far you have come in developing your skills. If you are jumping in here, I do not blame you, because these next few techniques push the fun meter pretty far.

The techniques in this chapter start and finish the same way. The application of the dye is very different. This paisley technique is intended to mimic rare and expensive paisley cloth; the result will feel as if someone has sent you a present. I am always excited to see how the student's react when these are opened.

A pastel or light value swatch works well in the paisley technique.

Gather:

- wool, a quarter yard swatch, pre-soaked in Synthrapol and 1 tablespoon CA crystals for 30 minutes
- 4-inch half hotel dye pan
- beakers
- dry dye powder for several colors
- squirt bottles
- plastic wrap
- aluminum foil
- Bluettes™ gloves

Paisley Technique: Oatmeal wool. Notice the more defined paisley shape. Starting with a pastel or light textured wool provides a built-in background color.

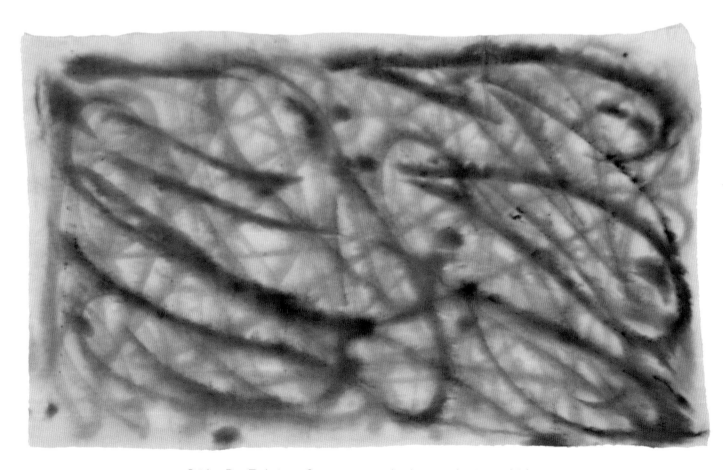

Paisley Dye Technique: One-quarter yard celery wool using multiple colors from squirt bottles. Void of any design plans... just play.

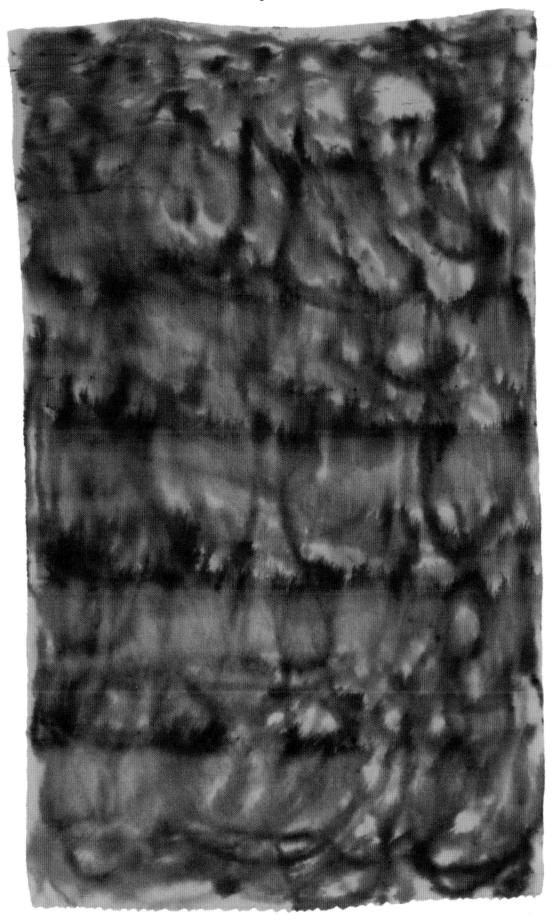

Paisley Technique: White wool. The results are always a surprise, and yummy. Some lines will blend together, others will not. This is one of my favorite examples of paisley.

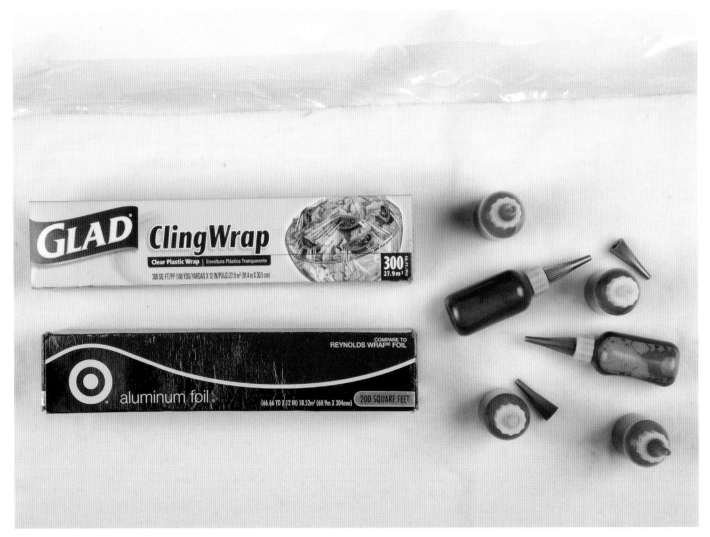

1. Paisley Dye Technique: Wool, pre-soaked in Synthrapol and CA crystals overnight, is resting on Glad® Cling Wrap. A variety of colors made with 1/2 to 1 teaspoon CA crystals dissolved into each beaker, cooled, and then poured into squirt bottles. A dye pan and the aluminum foil are used to finish the setting process.

Start:

- Make several colors in separate beakers.
- Add 1/2 teaspoon CA crystals.
- Add boiling water to dissolve the crystals and dry dye; stir well.
- Cool, then pour into squirt bottles. Vary the colors in value and intensity for best results.
- Lay the plastic wrap down on the counter, wider and longer than the size of your wool swatch. You may need to overlap several pieces of the clear wrap.
- Squeeze out excess water until very dry and lay the wool flat on top of the plastic wrap.
- Start by squirting the colors onto the wool in a variety of shapes and designs. I try to create a paisley design first and then build from there.

- When satisfied with your design, roll the bottom edge of the plastic wrap over the top of the wool and begin rolling like a cookie dough roll.
- Squeeze the ends together and twist.
- Tear off a piece of foil longer than your roll; wrap the rolled wool into the foil, then secure the ends.
- Place the roll in the dye pan and add water until one-third full.
- Cover and simmer, without boiling, for one hour.
- With your gloves on, remove the roll from the pan, place it in the sink, and cool with water.
- Carefully remove the foil and cut both ends of the plastic wrap to open.
- The wool will unravel from the plastic wrap.
- Wash with detergent, rinse well, and dry.

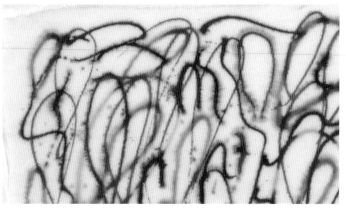

4. The wool is covered with color in random paisley shapes. This wool may be cut horizontally or vertically for great accents in projects.

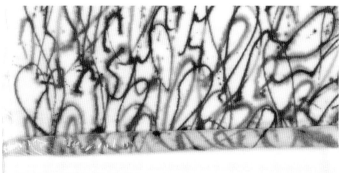

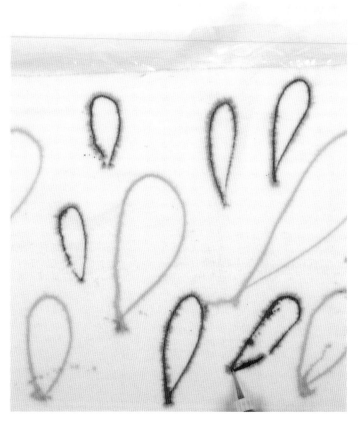

2. Begin by squirting the paisley shape onto the wool. This will establish the essence of a paisley fabric design. The squirt bottles are then used randomly to fill the wool swatch with patterns.

5. Once finished with the color application, the bottom edge of the plastic wrap is folded onto the bottom edge of the wool to begin the roll, protecting the paisley design on the wool.

6. The paisley roll is wrapped in aluminum foil and the ends are secured.

3. Very little pressure is needed to squirt the shape onto the wool. PRO Chemical & Dye Inc.®, golden cap squirt bottles are great for this technique. Some lines are thicker than others in this view.

7. Secured, the roll is placed into the dye pan with water and covered. The dye pan will simmer, without boiling, for one hour. Use caution when unwrapping; they may be very hot. Wash with detergent, rinse well and dry. Enjoy!

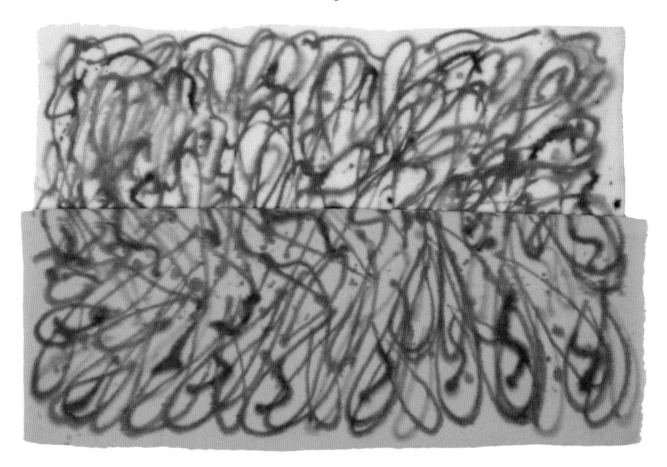

The same colors on two different starting wools. The color does spread slightly in this technique, but starting with the driest possible swatch decreases the potential for colors to merge.

The combinations of color are endless and the results always unique. The results amaze me. When the wool is used in traditional hand hooking it mimics original paisley and adds a spark. All wool stashes need a little brightness. I consider this like a poison in my stash...you do not need much.

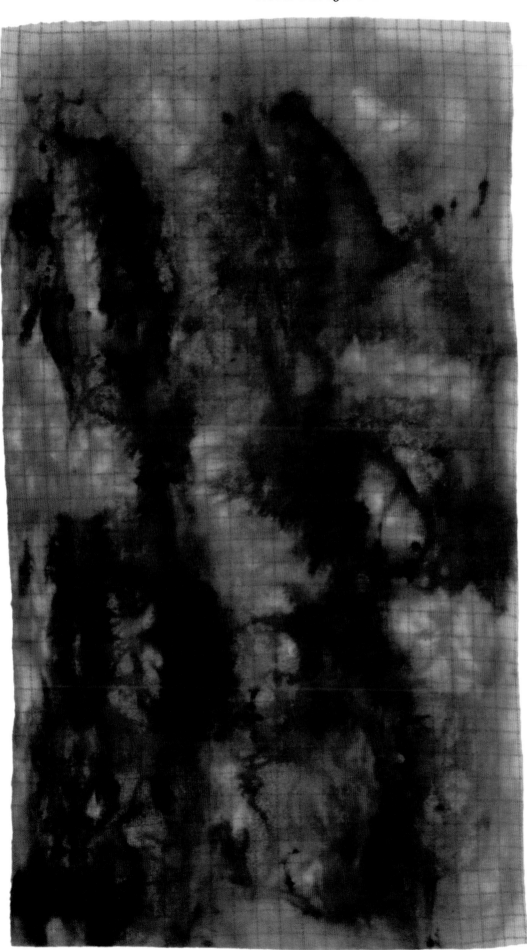

This textured wool shows how much the color may spread in the setting process. It may be due to the pre-soaking time in citric acid, as increased pre-soaking time may prevent this. The original wool is still visible top right. *Wool donated by Pat Cross.*

Dry Dye Technique: White wool. The blues and purples appear to be dancing on the wool. This technique is like opening a present every time you use it.

Dry Dye Technique with textured wool. The combination of texture and dry dye make these very exciting. The original wool pattern offers another element to any project. *Wool donated by Pat Cross*

DRY DYE TECHNIQUE

The results of this technique always receive the most attention. There is never a guarantee how it will look, but I have never witnessed disappointment. This technique starts and finishes like the paisley and painted techniques.

There are unlimited possibilities for the finished wool using this technique. It is hard to describe the unbelievable explosion of color. This is yet another way to deposit color onto wool for interest and excitement. Have a great time with it.

Gather:

- wool, a quarter yard swatch, pre-soaked in Synthrapol and 1 tablespoon CA crystals for 30 minutes
- 4-inch half hotel dye pan
- dry dye powder
- salt shakers
- salt
- plastic wrap
- aluminum foil
- Bluettes™ gloves

Start:

- Add the desired amount of dry dye powder to empty salt shakers. I recommend one color per shaker. I vary the dry dye amounts by filling the shakers between 1/16 and 1/8 full with dry dye and, then, topping them off with salt.

- With the salt shaker lid on securely, cover the top with a paper towel and shake until the dry dye and salt are mixed well. Set aside.

- Lay the plastic wrap out on the counter, wider and longer than the size of the wool swatch. You may need to overlap several pieces of the clear wrap.

- Squeeze out excess water and lay the wool flat on top of the plastic wrap.

- Sprinkle the dye mixture on the wool. Go sparingly at first, until you have experienced the results. Shaking too hard or heavily leaves a blurred result.

- When satisfied with your design, roll the bottom edge of the plastic wrap over the bottom edge of the wool and begin rolling like a cookie dough roll.

137

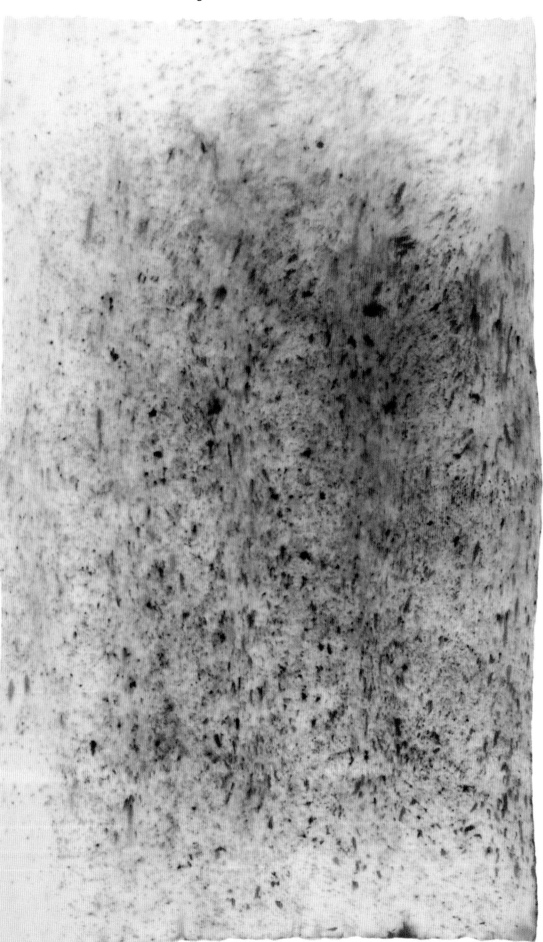

Using white or natural wool allows the true color of the dye particles to show and often the show is unbelievable. Amazing!

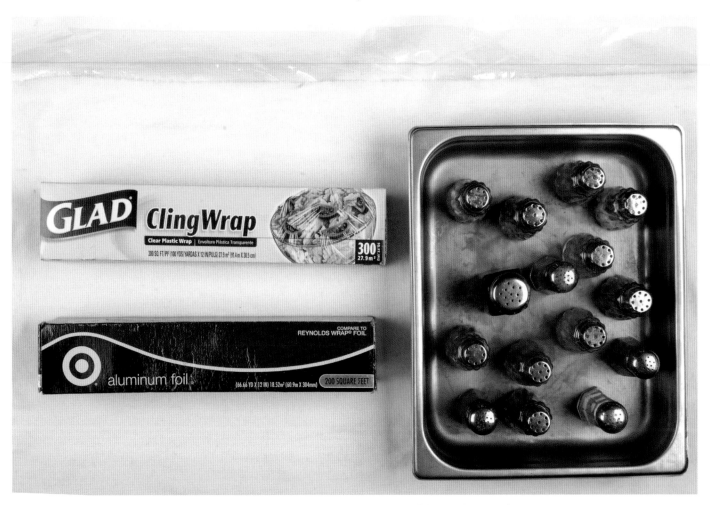

1. Dry Dye Technique: Wool, pre-soaked in Synthrapol and CA crystals overnight, resting on the plastic wrap, salt shakers with dry dye powder and salt, dye pan, and aluminum foil.

- Squeeze the ends together and twist.
- Tear off a piece of aluminum foil longer than your roll and wrap the roll into the foil, securing the ends.
- Place the roll in the pan and fill the pan one-third full of water.
- Cover and simmer, without boiling, for one hour.
- With gloves on, remove the roll from the pan, place it into the sink, and cool with water.
- Carefully remove the foil and cut both ends of the plastic wrap to open. The wool will unravel from the plastic wrap.
- Wash with detergent, rinse well, and dry.

2. The wool is not too dry. Lightly shake the dry dye powder mixed with salt randomly onto the wool. Too much shaking results in a muddy swatch or dark value.

4. Fold the plastic wrap over the bottom edge of the wool, and then roll the entire swatch like cookie dough going into the freezer. This protects the dry dye particles on the swatch as much as possible.

3. The moisture in the wool allows some of the dry dye to become visible. Less is more here. Have fun with it.

5. The rolled swatch is then wrapped in foil, protecting the wool and keeping the plastic from melting. Secure the ends tightly. In a pan, simmer, without boiling, for one hour. Use caution when unwrapping. Wash with detergent, rinse well, and dry. Most of all enjoy.

Dry Dye Technique: One-quarter yard textured wool, several salt and dye shakers. Using medium value textured wool will provide a less intense swatch. The original pattern is an added benefit.

Visibly this shows the reason to use light shakes of the salt shaker with the dry dye powder and salt. Nonetheless it is a lovely surprise. Great color combinations, and no two are alike!

It is easier to visualize the wool and how it would look in a traditional hooking project if it is crumpled together.

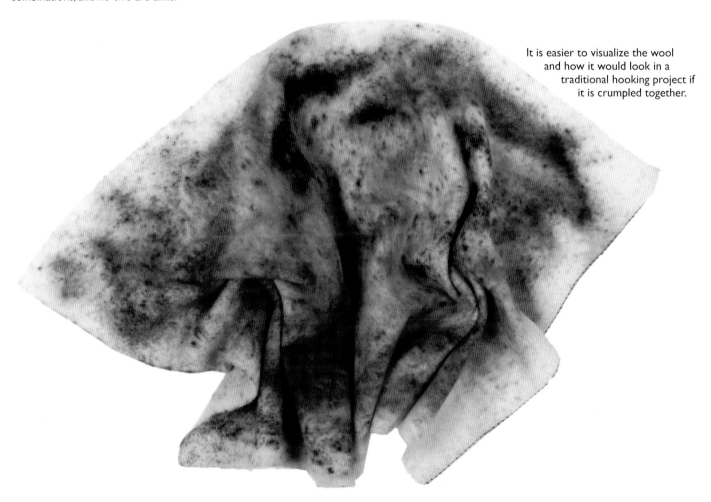

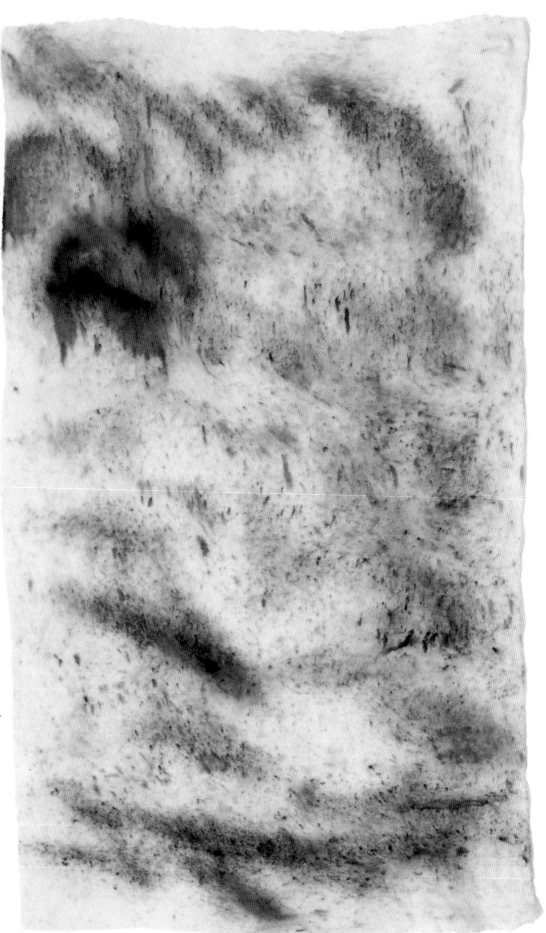

Dry Dye Technique: White wool. If the results are too intense, an overdye with a very weak solution of the direct complement is a great way to dull the color slightly. I always need at least one of the intense wools around.

Dry Dye Technique: One-quarter yard sunyellow wool. Again the use of several salt and dye shakers on pastel or other light colored wools is great. The wool surprises are the best.

Dry Dye Technique: One-quarter yard natural wool. Several, salt/dye shakers were used, and the purple was a lot of fun. Heavy shakes allow more dye to fall onto the wool. Put the colors you love in the salt shakers and it can only be yummy, every time.

Dry Dye, Paisley, and Painted Techniques blend well together. The color placement on the wools combined with these techniques create a great deal of movement and excitement in the wools.

This vase holds wools from the Paisley, Floating Dry Dye, and Open Pan Techniques. Color relationships are relative to surrounding colors. In this group there is light, bright, dark, and dull, the pink paisley becomes the poison.

FINDING PURPLE!

The secondary color purple is below the color blue on the value scale. In mixing and blending color, it requires only a little measure of purple dry dye for changes to occur. Different hues of purple come from a variety of reds and blues.

Spend some time mixing the primary colors to make purple. Try mixing true blue with pastel red to make purple. This will build on your ability to mix colors and also strengthen your "dye by eye" skills. Yes, have a purple day.

The dye lessons in this chapter are what I consider to be more advanced techniques. The basics have been learned and the focus is now on how much manipulation is applied to the wool prior to the dye reaching it. Some of the techniques are variations or combinations of those learned earlier in this book. I am sure you will find favorites.

COLOR OVERLAY TECHNIQUE

This technique is the one I use every time I need to clean my dye kitchen. When I leave color in beakers waiting to be used, this is where they end up. The layers of color created every time you add a different color to the dye pan are very exciting. The key is to have the CA crystals dissolved in the dye pan first.

Select colors that avoid making mud. Analogous warm or cool colors work well in one dye pan. Golden colors are great and not much could go wrong here, so enjoy. Mix several purples and try having a purple day!

Gather:

- wool, quarter yard swatches, pre-soaked for 30 minutes in Synthrapol.
- 4-inch half hotel dye pan
- several beakers
- dry dye powder or leftover color
- CA crystals
- Synthrapol
- salt (optional)
- Bluettes™ gloves

Color Overlay Technique: One-quarter yard each of oatmeal and natural wool. Color overlay adds levels of color to one piece of wool. Colors used: [490, 1/16], [490, 1/32] + [119, 1/16], [845, 1/8], and leftover blue + purple mud in separate beakers. Analogous colors work great here.

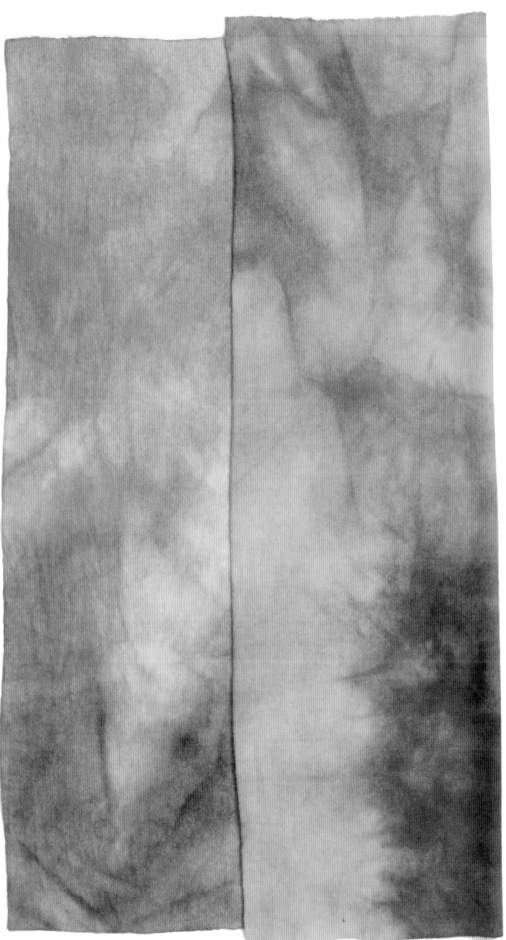

Color Overlay Technique: One-quarter yard each of oatmeal, grey, tan, with natural and celery wool. Natural wool is on the left and celery on the right. Colors used: [490, 1/16], [490, 1/32 + 119, 1/16], [845, 1/8], and blue and purple mud in separate beakers.

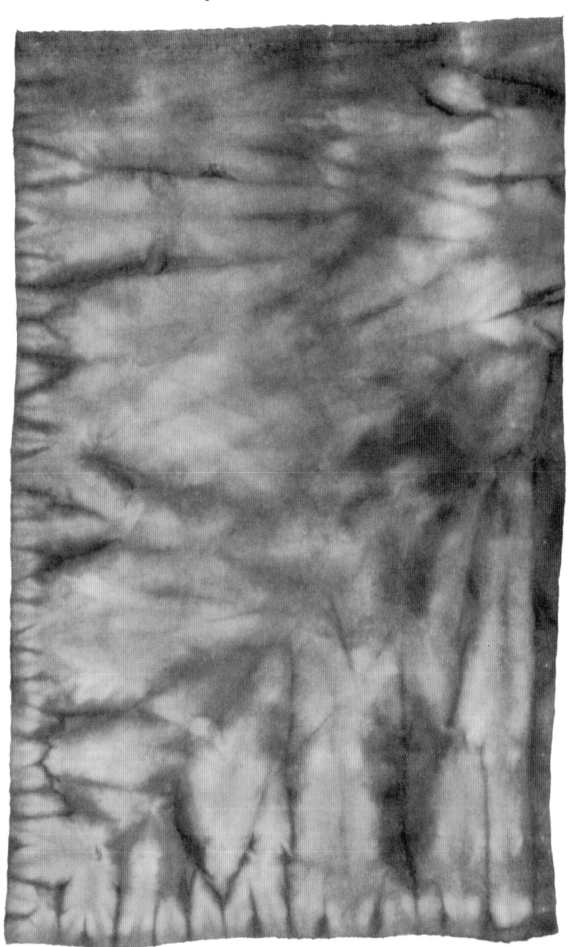

The Color Overlay Technique may even be used in Shibori Techniques. There are no limits, but, if you forget that CA crystals go into the dye pan first, you will find only mud.

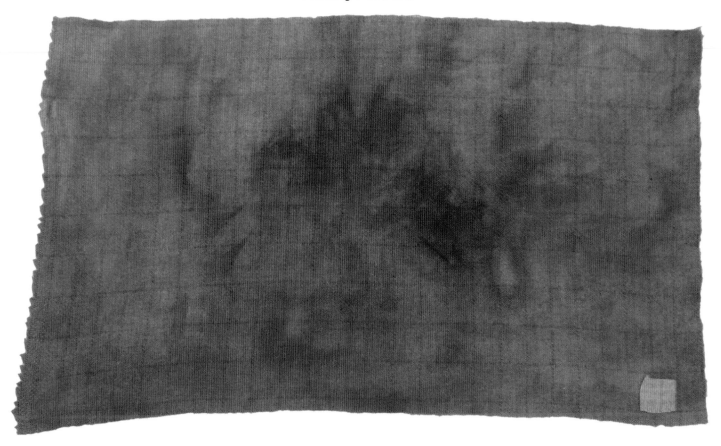

Color Overlay Technique starting with a textured wool. The small sample bottom right represents the original wool's color and pattern. After dyeing, the pattern is still visible and adds dimension. *Wool donated by Pat Cross.*

Start:

- Fill dye pan two-thirds full of water.

- Add 1 tablespoon CA crystals and simmer, without boiling, to dissolve crystals.

- Make several dye baths or use what may be sitting around.

- Squeeze the excess water from the wool and place it in the dye pan.

- Starting with the brightest color, with gloves on, lift the wool out of the pan, pour the color in, and then replace the wool.

- Wait for the water to clear of color and repeat.

- Remove the wool with a gloved hand and pour in the next color.

- Immerse the wool and leave it until the water clears. This process is continued until you reach the desired value and color.

- Simmer, without boiling, for one hour.

- Wash with detergent, rinse well, and dry.

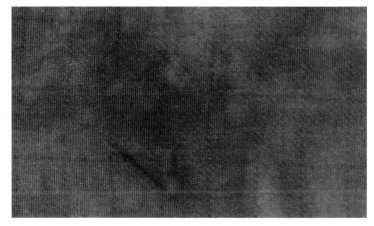

Detail.

1. Color Overlay Technique: Several colors in separate beakers, pre-soaked wool in the dye pan with water and 1 tablespoon CA crystals dissolved.

2. With a gloved hand, lift the wool out of the dye pan, pour in the first color, then immerse the wool back into the dye pan. I prefer to use the lightest or brightest color first.

4. The second color has been added once the water was clear. The CA crystals in the dye pan move the color into the wool faster. Highlights and lowlights develop as the color is applied.

3. Use patience here. The dye needs to go into the wool before adding the second color.

5. The wool is again lifted from the pan to add the third color. Continue this process until all the colors have been added to the dye pan. Simmer, without boiling, for one hour, then wash with detergent, rinse well and dry.

Color Overlay Technique on a Glen Plaid. This is my favorite technique when I need to clean up the dye kitchen. This allows for so many color combinations to add dimension and fascination to wool.

Color Overlay Technique: The overlay of color is more visible here. You are able to see how the colors appear to lay one on top of the other. This is what makes this dye process so much fun.

Color Overlay Technique: One-quarter yard natural wool. Colors used: [478, 1/8], [425, 1/2] + [502, 1/32], and [490, 1/8] in separate beakers. The relative lightest color will go into the dye pan first.

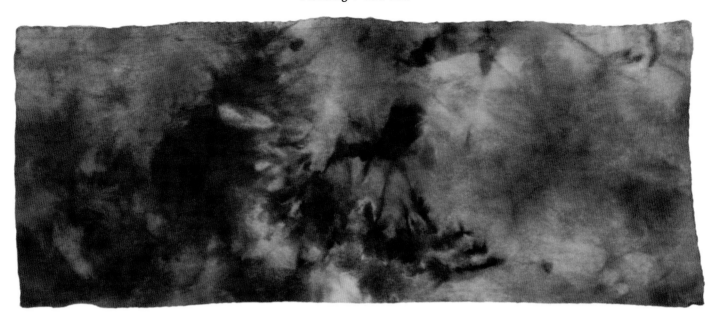

Color Overlay Technique: One-quarter yard of natural wool. Colors used: [502, 1/16], [119, 1/16] + [351, 1/32] + [490, 1/128], [672, 1/16] (as needed), [502 + 672], and leftover dye bath as needed. We need neutral colors to balance our wool stash and allow a place for our eyes to rest.

Color Overlay Technique: One-quarter yard each of grey, natural, celery, and tan wool. Colors used: [502, 1/16], [119, 1/16] + [351, 1/32] + [490, 1/128], and [672, 1/16] in separate beakers. Any color leftover in my dye kitchen is fair game.

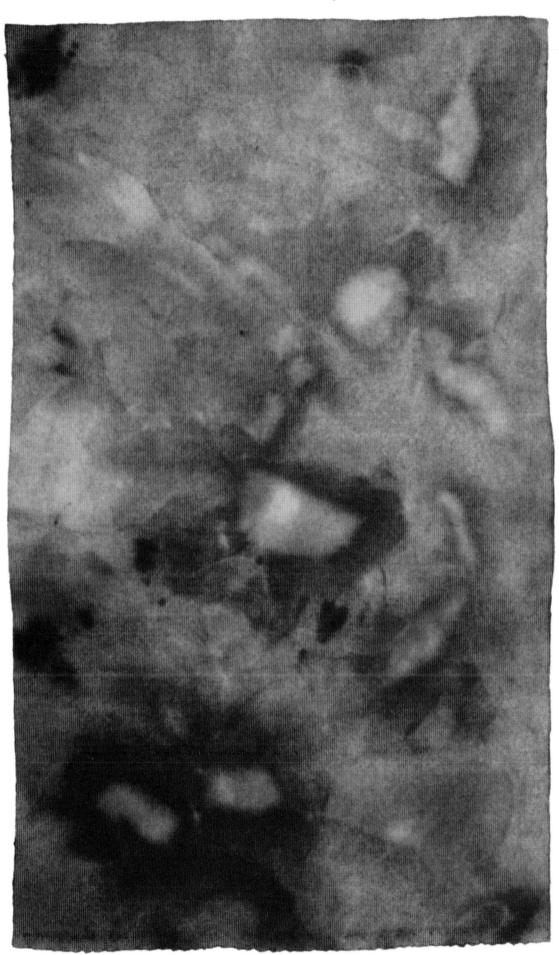

With leftover colors this technique works best using relative lightest or brightest to darkest color.

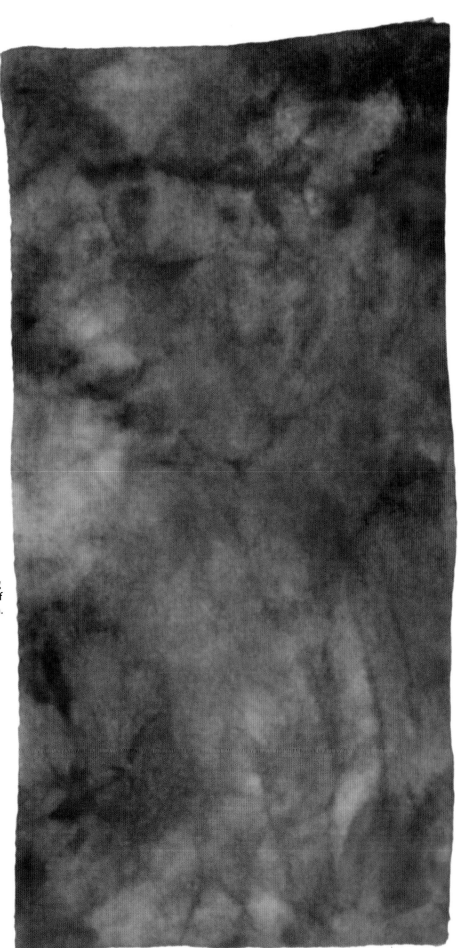

Another result of leftover color on a dye day. This is a great time to practice dyeing by eye. Pour a little or all of the leftover dye into the pan.

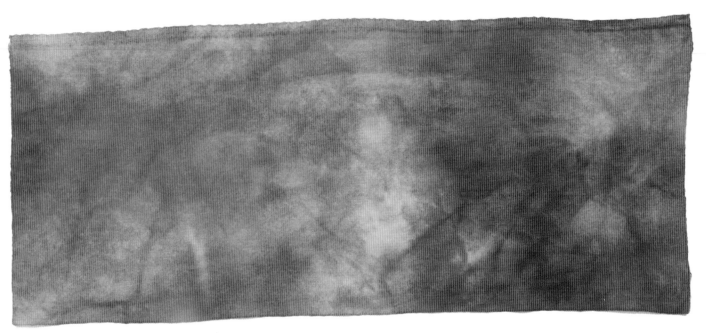

Color Overlay Technique: One-quarter yard of natural wool. Colors used: [119, 1/16], [233, 1/32], and [351, 1/64] in separate beakers. Bright colors may be darkened by adding small amounts of black.

Color Overlay Technique: One-quarter yard each of oatmeal, tan, celery, sunyellow, and natural wool. Colors used: [340, 1/8], [119, 1/4], and [338, 1/8] in separate beakers, including leftover orange red. It does not get any warmer than this!

FLOATING DRY DYE TECHNIQUE

We are building on the previous techniques of floating color onto the wool, this time with dry dye in salt shakers. Here the wool floats and the dry dye and salt is sprinkled onto the wool.

In this technique, you are watching the dry dye particles land or drift, leaving a trail of color and texture. The value does change slightly, but I find it adds to the dimension of color here.

Gather:

- wool, a quarter yard or desired amount, pre-soaked in Synthrapol
- 4-inch half hotel pan
- salt shakers
- dry dye
- CA crystals
- Synthrapol
- salt (optional)
- Bluettes™ gloves

The Floating Dry Dye Technique is beautiful. The dry dye looks as though it had been dusted onto the wool. This sample shows how the dye dances on the wool prior to settling in place. It also demonstrates how colors surrounding one another affect the overall harmony, like the wool against the orange flowers and the dark brown vase.

1. Floating Dry Dye Technique: salt shakers with salt and dry dye powder, dye pan with heated water, dissolved CA crystals, pre-soaked wool in the dye pan ready to float dry dye.

Floating Dry Dye Technique
enhances the original wool.
The original value of the
starting wool is considered
when making color choices.

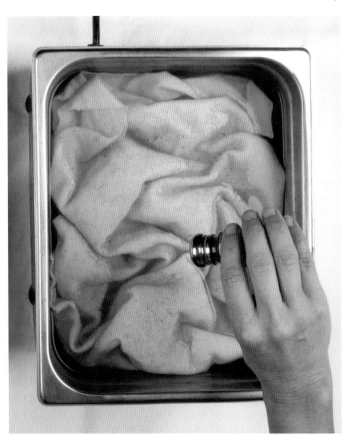

2. Shake a small amount of dye onto the wool and allow the particles to float. Avoid the urge to move the wool. The dry dye will settle into the wool after a minute or two.

4. Once the visible area is dyed carefully shift the wool in the pan and start to add more colors on the undyed area.

3. Continue to gently shake the color on the wool. It will drift and float once the color settles on the wool. Shake until happy.

5. When satisfied, simmer the wool, without boiling, for one hour. Wash with detergent, rinse well and dry. Enjoy!

Start:

- Fill the dye pan two-thirds full of water.

- Add 1 tablespoon CA crystals and simmer, without boiling, to dissolve crystals.

- Prepare your salt shakers by adding desired amount of dry dye powder to empty salt shakers. I recommend one color per shaker. I vary the dry dye amounts by filling the shakers between 1/16 and 1/8 full with dry dye and topping them off with salt.

- With the salt shaker lid secured, cover the top with a paper towel and shake until the dry dye and salt are mixed well. Set aside.

- Squeeze excess water from the wool.

- Place the wool into the dye pan creating hills and valleys.

- Using one salt shaker at a time, sprinkle the dry dye onto the hills and valleys allowing the dye particles to float onto the wool. Some of the dye particles will travel. Give the particles time to rest on the wool.

- Add from the next shaker of color and allow time for the dye particles to stay on the wool.

- After a few shakers, you may decide to move your wool around to reach undyed areas. Recreate your hills and valleys and continue to sprinkle dye until

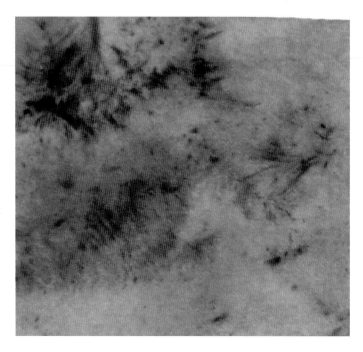

you have the look you want. There is no right or wrong here.

- After the last shaker, simmer, without boiling, for one hour.

- Wash with detergent, rinse well, and dry.

Floating Dry Dye Technique: One-quarter yard of natural wool using multiple salt/dye shakers.
The hills and valleys in the wool take up the dry dye as other particles slightly overdye the wool.

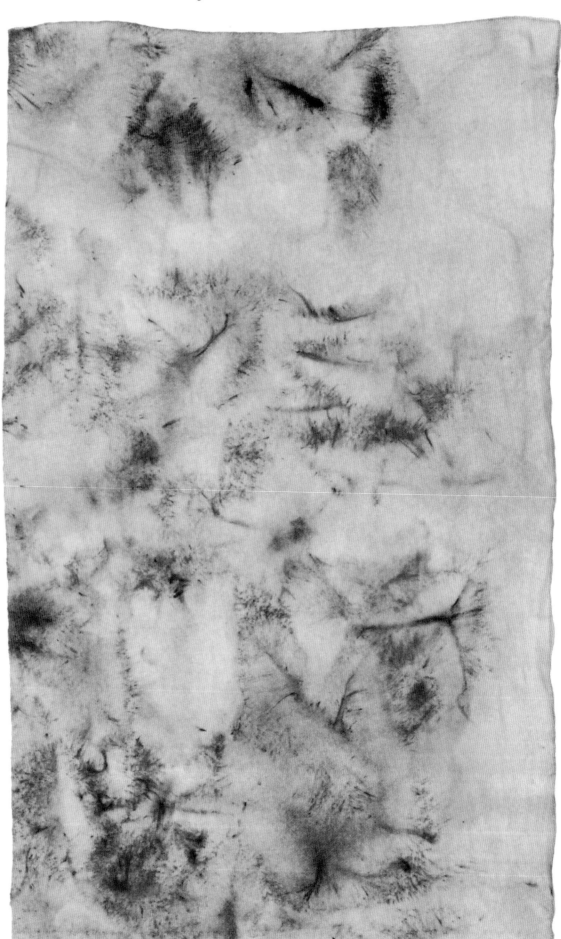

Floating Dry Dye Technique: One-quarter yard, natural wool, multiple salt/dye shakers used here. These are so exciting and the possibilities are endless.

Floating Dry Dye Technique:
One-quarter yard of natural
wool using several salt/dye
shakers. This is an easy way to
change the color or texture in
a piece of wool.

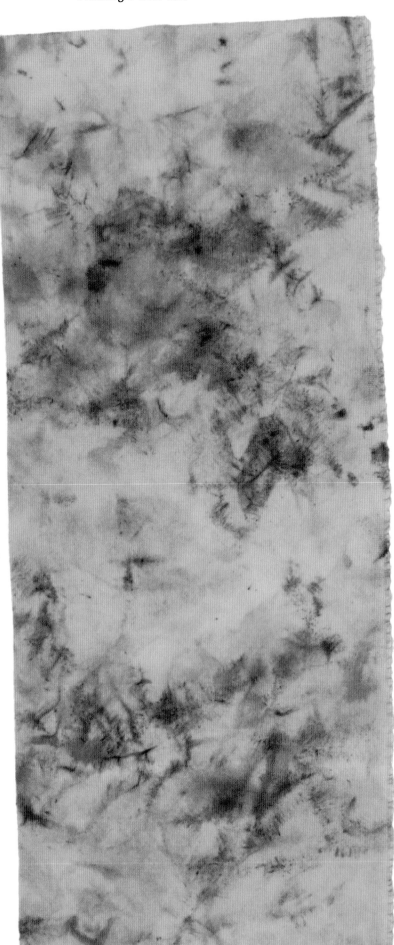

Floating Dry Dye Technique: One-quarter yard of natural wool and the colors from several, salt/dye shakers. This is one of my favorite color combinations: secondary orange, purple, and green.

Floating Dry Dye Technique: One-quarter yard of celery wool. Several salt/dye shakers were used, but more colors were from the warm side of the color wheel.

Floating Dry Dye Technique: One-quarter yard each of natural, grey, sunyellow, and oatmeal wool. With little in common in the beginning, the wool swatches now share the same color and may be used together.

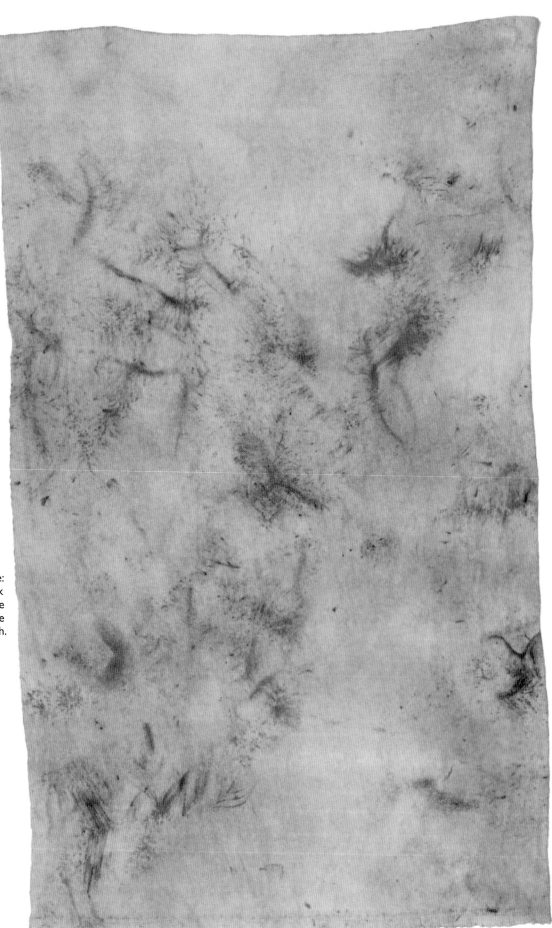

Floating Dry Dye Technique:
Analogous color plans work
well in this technique. There
is always just a little surprise
in each swatch.

ROCKS AND WOOL TECHNIQUE

This technique is a great deal of fun. It reminds me of making mud pies as a little girl. The rocks act as a resist to the dye on the wool and it is always surprising how the color settles into the wool.

I really find the results striking. I experimented with a spotdye and this technique, using exactly the same colors. I found the color deposited on the wool in this technique to be much more extreme in values than the spotdye.

Gather:

- wool, a quarter yard, pre-soaked for 30 minutes in Synthrapol.
- a small enamel or stainless steel dye pot with a handle
- 2 or 3 beakers
- dry dye powder, 2 or 3 colors
- small, decorative rocks
- CA crystals
- Synthrapol
- salt (optional)
- Bluettes™ gloves,

Rocks and Wool Technique: One-quarter yard, grey, and one-quarter yard celery wool. Colors used: [351, 1/16] + [560, 1/32] and [351-1/8] in separate beakers. This technique creates high contrast both in color and value.

Dyed wool hangs to dry in the Greenhouse at Vermont Technical College, the perfect setting to teach a dye class. Zina Howe, is the Greenhouse Technician and Adjunct Faculty responsible for the beautiful flowers in the picture.

The tight fit results in extreme value changes for this amazing technique. Using leftover dye, this reminds me of the sun shining through the leaves, one of my absolute favorite results. It is in my private collection.

Rocks and Wool
Dye Technique:
One-quarter yard of
celery wool. Colors
used: Forest Green
[725, 1/32] + [119,
1/16]. The success
depends on a tight
fit between the
rocks, wool, and the
dye pan.

Start:

- Make your color in separate beakers.
- Add 1-1/2 teaspoon CA crystals to each beaker.
- Dissolve dry dye powder, and crystals with boiling water.
- Place a few rocks into the bottom of the dye pot; this prevents the wool from burning.
- Squeeze excess water from wool.
- Place the wool into the pan and start overlapping the wool and rocks in a random fashion. Pack the wool and rocks tightly, then pile a few rocks on top.
- Pour the first color onto the wool in a random fashion. Consideration must be given to the amount of liquid being added to the pot.
- Pour the next color randomly onto the wool. Continue until all of the colors are used.
- If necessary, add additional water to the pot to disperse the color and prevent the wool from burning.
- Simmer, without boiling, for one hour.
- With a glove on, pour the wool and rocks into the sink
- Rinse the rocks and separate.
- Wash the wool with detergent, rinse well and dry.

Detail of the photo on previous page.

1. Rocks and Wool Dye Technique: a small dye pot, pre-soaked wool, rocks, 1 to 3 colors with 1 teaspoon CA crystals dissolved in each beaker. Rocks are place in the pan bottom.

2. The wool and remaining rocks are intertwined together, packing both tightly into the dye pot.

4. The second color is added randomly. The pan will fill quickly as the wool is surrounded by color.

3. The first color is added randomly onto the wool, allow the dye to drain through the layers of rock and wool.

5. Add the final color and check the water level in the pan. Simmer, without boiling, for one hour. Wash with detergent, rinse well and dry. It is a surprise!

Rocks and Wool Dye Technique has its own uniqueness, different from spotdyed wool. The rocks act as a resist for the dye while creating really amazing and fun results.

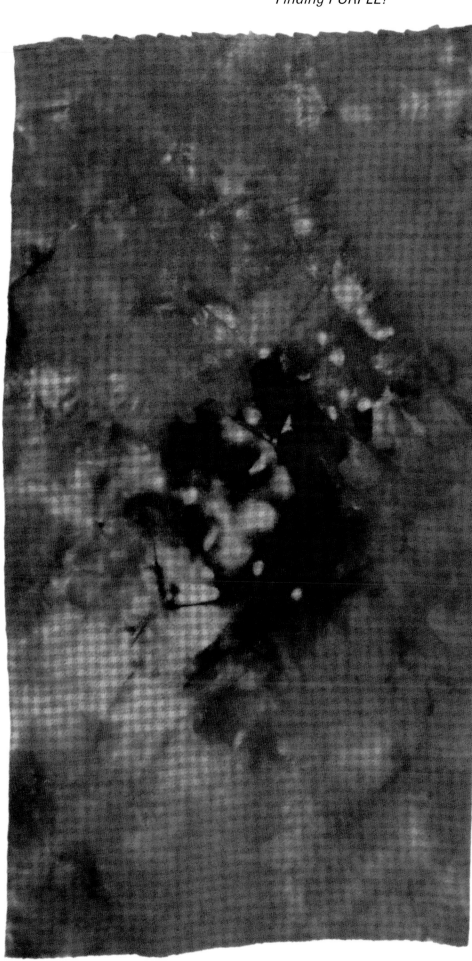

Rocks and Wool Dye Technique with textured wool. The values are less extreme when starting with textured wool, but the original pattern is a bonus..
Courtesy of Pat Cross.

Rocks and Wool Dye Technique: One-quarter yard of tan wool. Colors used: [440, 1/64], [490, 1/64], and [672, 1/64] in separate beakers. I like to begin with light value wool. The results are another dimensional surprise.

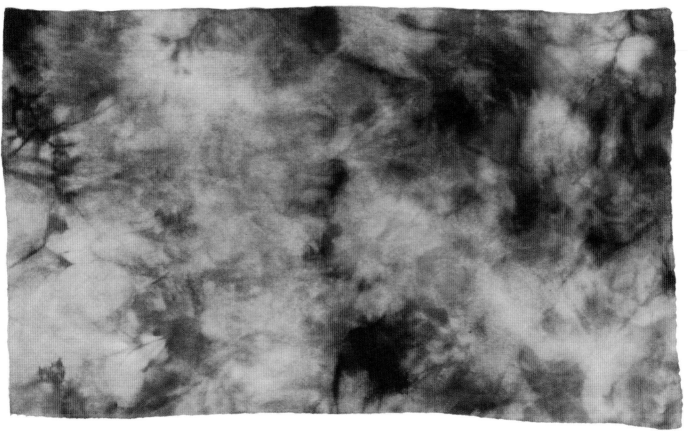

Rocks and Wool Dye Technique: One-quarter yard of natural wool. Colors used: [119, 1/16], [351, 1/32], and [490, 1/128] in separate beakers. This may be considered a color party or a little poison in my stash.

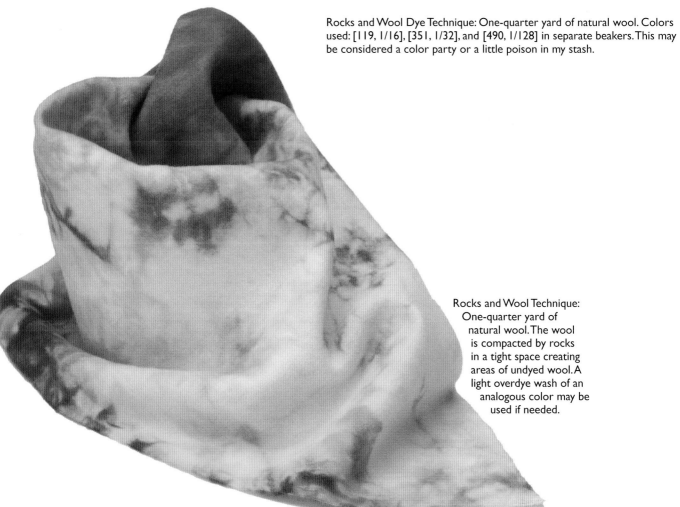

Rocks and Wool Technique: One-quarter yard of natural wool. The wool is compacted by rocks in a tight space creating areas of undyed wool. A light overdye wash of an analogous color may be used if needed.

FABRIC MANIPULATIONS

The techniques in this chapter come from the Japanese tradition of Shibori. While silk was used in Japan in many beautiful ways, it is not difficult to adapt the techniques to wool. The wool is folded, wrapped, and/or stitched to make areas of resist to the dye deposited onto the wool.

The following techniques are only a few of the endless possibilities used to manipulate the wool into different shapes before adding color. Many floral departments carry the necessary tools, such as glass cubes, rocks, floral wire, and other interesting shapes. Again, experiment and have fun.

SHIBORI FOLDING TECHNIQUE

The folding technique is like folding paper or even napkin folding. The wool may be folded into any shape or several shapes in one swatch. For example, you may consider a fan fold, followed by a roll. The square fold and triangle fold are among several I have played with.

The following techniques start with dry wool; it is easier to work with it. Pastel wools work great and light value textured wool is also very nice. The textured wool has been very successful in retaining the original pattern. These are quick, and easy.

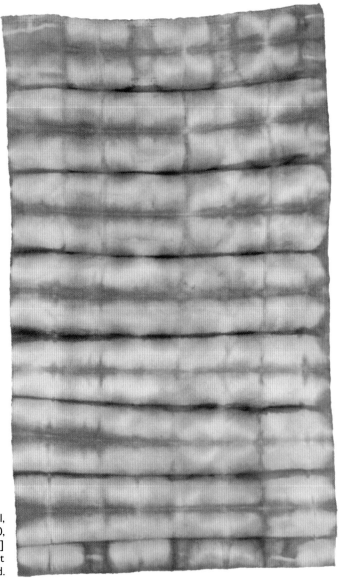

Shibori Folding Technique: One-quarter yard of sunyellow wool, folded fan style then squared. Colors used: [119, 1/16] + [490, 1/128], Evergreen, [729, 1/128], and [503, 1/128] + [199, 1/32] in separate beakers. This reminds me of bamboo. It may be cut vertically or horizontally, depending on need. It may even be framed.

I designed this, "Beginner Patchwork" rug for two reasons. One was to teach an adult learning class through the University of Louisville. The second reason was to use wools dyed specifically using Shibori, Color Overlay, Dry Dye, and Over Dye Techniques.

Shibori Folding Technique: One-quarter yard of tan wool on top, using a fan fold. Colors used: [340, 1/16], [366, 1/32], [819, 1/64], and [819, 1/128] at the end, all in separate beakers. The green swatch using a pole wrap is one-quarter yard of tan wool. Colors used: [413, 1/64], [440, 1/64]; these are unwrapped then [413, 1/64] is added, with a squirt of [119] from a condiment bottle.

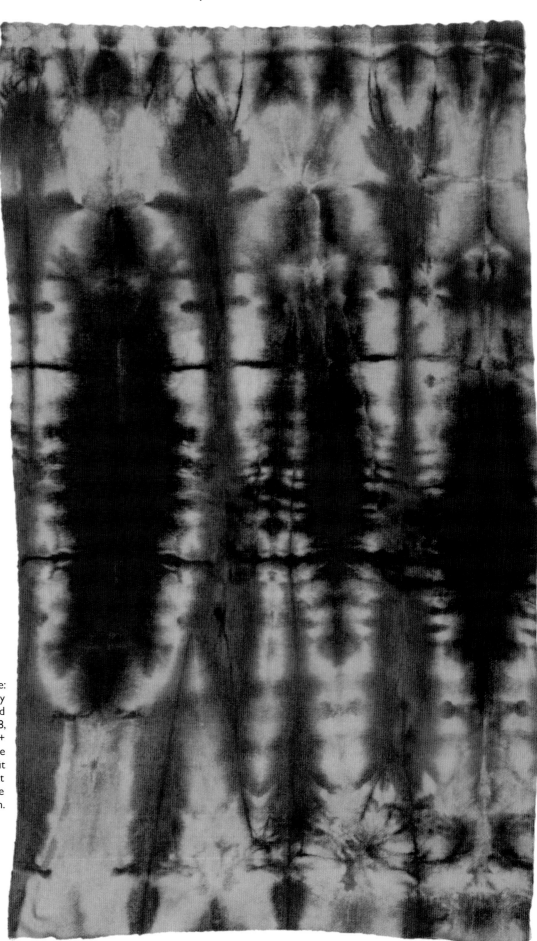

Shibori Folding Technique: One-quarter yard of grey wool. This was fan rolled with colors: Purple [918, 1/32] and [818, 1/32] + [351, 1/64], in separate beakers. Who knew it could be such fun? Great for the cool side of the color wheel stash.

Gather:

- wool, a dry, quarter yard swatch
- small enamel pot with a handle or 2-inch half hotel dye pan
- 2 beakers
- dry dye powder, 2 colors
- twine, string, floral wire, and large safety pins
- CA crystals
- Synthrapol
- Bluettes™ gloves

Start:

- Fill the dye pan one-third full of water, Synthrapol, and 1 tablespoon CA crystals.
- Simmer, without boiling, to dissolve the crystals.
- Make your colors in separate beakers; there is no limit to the number of colors.

- On a flat surface, fold your dry wool in whatever way you choose.
- Pin, tie, or string the folded wool in place.
- Place the folded wool into the dye pan and allow the water to absorb into the folded wool.
- Pour the first color into the dye pan. You may decide to pour the color directly on the wool, as the placement of color in the pan creates the magic in the end. If you plan to turn your wool over, and repeat the application on the other side, you might only use half of your dye bath on each side.
- When ready, add the next color into the pan or, again, directly on the wool.
- When the water is clear add more water to two-thirds of the height of the wool.
- Simmer, without boiling, for one hour and cool.
- With gloves on, untie, unwrap, or unpin.
- Wash with detergent, rinse well, and dry.

1. Shibori Folding Technique: dry wool, folded and secured, Synthrapol in the dye pan with CA crystals dissolved in the heated water. Several colors with the CA crystals, dissolved into the dye bath. The dry wool may be secured with twine, safety pins, or other non-flammable items.

2.

3.

4.

2. The wool is placed in the pan where the Synthrapol wets the wool. Turn the wool to be sure the entire swatch is wet. Add the color as you like, around the wool or directly on top of the folds. It is all wonderful.

3. Add the second color randomly.

4. It is fine to add dissolved CA crystals into the dye pan or in the dye bath. The wool may be turned over for added contrast in the results. Simmer, without boiling, for one hour. With smaller pans the water level must be checked frequently. Wash with detergent, rinse well, and dry.

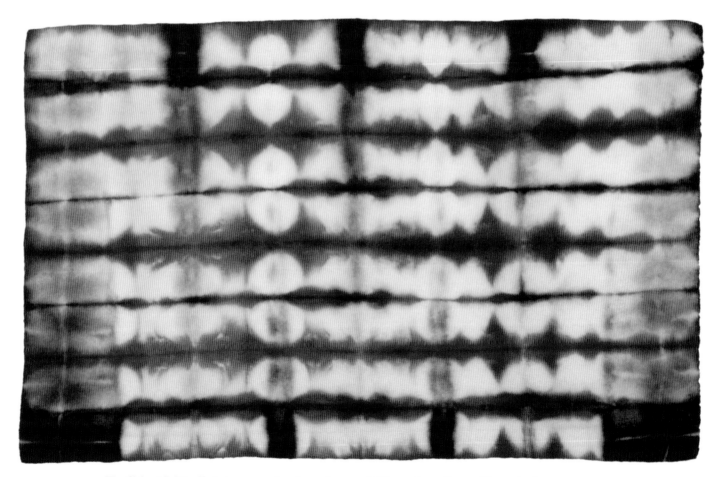

The Shibori Folding Techniques are stunning and easy as folding a piece of paper. The undyed areas are created by the folds and the application of dye. A light analogous overdye may be used if desired.

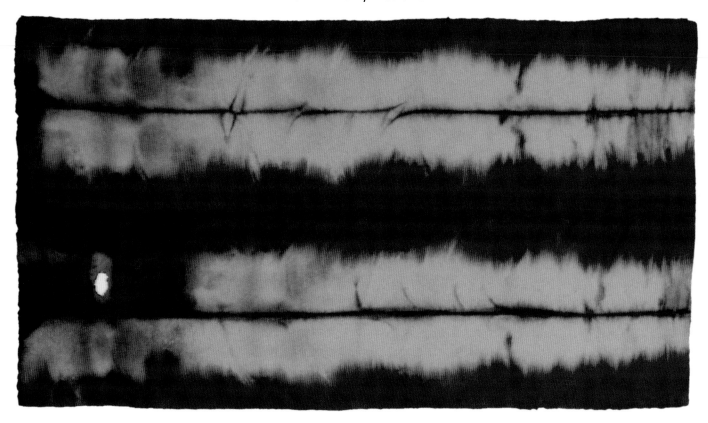

Shibori Folding Technique: Starting with grey wool or other light colored wool creates areas of resist. As the dye is applied a pattern emerges and the original wool color adds instead of detracts from the results. I sometimes transfer things to a stew pan, not enough water in this one burning a hole in the wool., bottom left

Left: 1. The Shibori Folding Technique: rolled wool is immersed in color. The water in the dye pan contains Synthrapol and CA crystals. The second color is ready.

Above: 2. The second color is added to the pan and the wool is turned over. Simmer one hour, wash with detergent, rinse well, and dry. Enjoy!

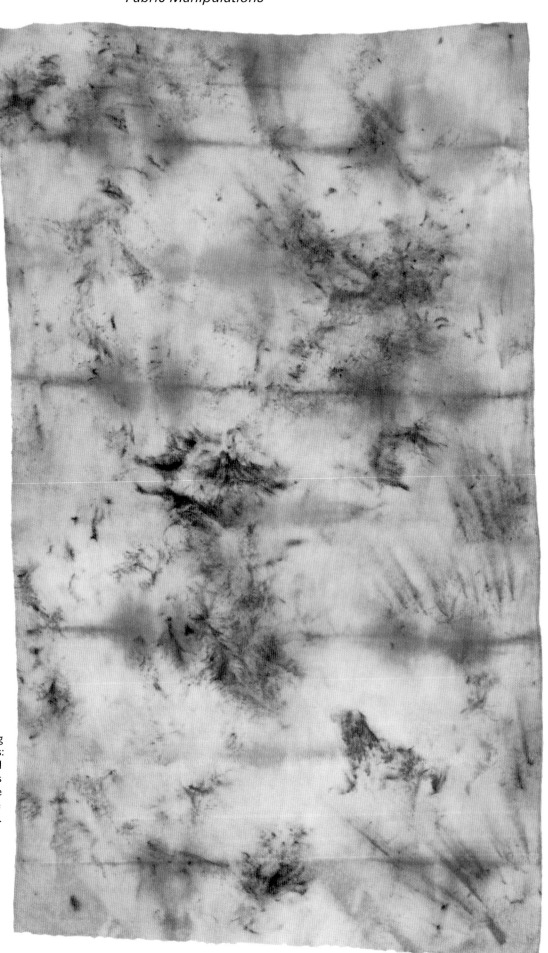

Shibori Folding and Floating Dry Dye Techniques: Color. [490, 1/128] and several salt and dye shakers were used during the technique. Many of these techniques may be combined.

182

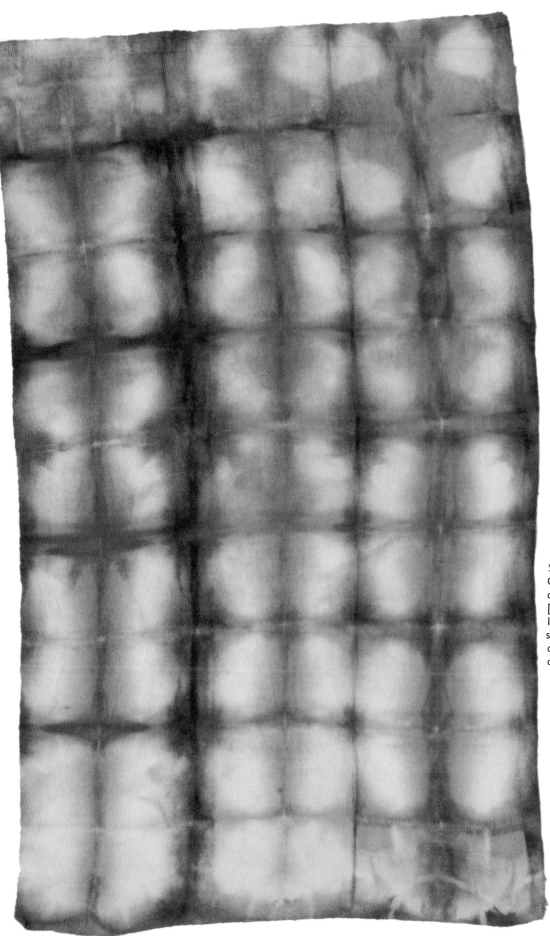

Shibori Folding Technique: One-quarter yard of celery wool. Colors: [478, 1/128], [119, 1/16], and [351, 1/64] in separate beakers. This color combination is one of my favorites.

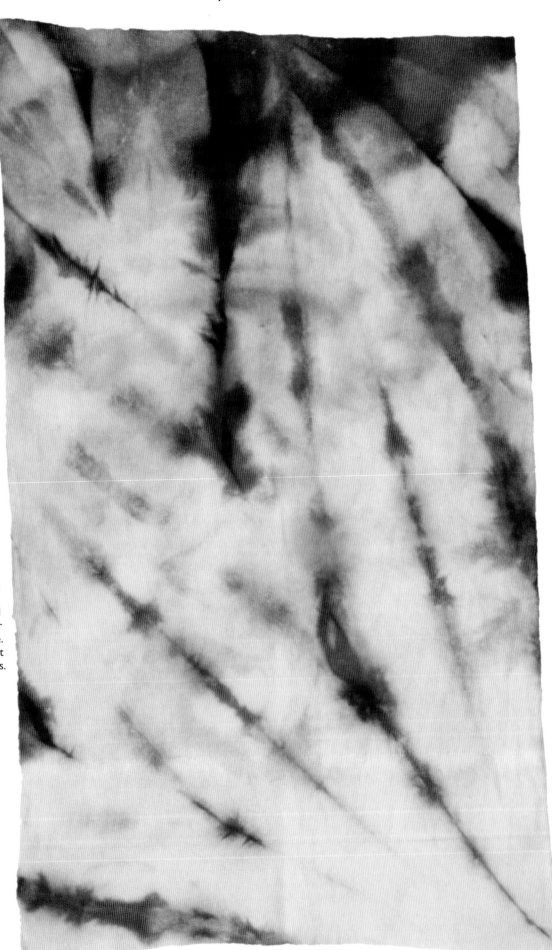

Shibori Folding Technique: One-quarter yard of natural wool, using [119], [490], and [351] dyes. Sparks of color cover the wool like a wave. Every fold will offer different and great results.

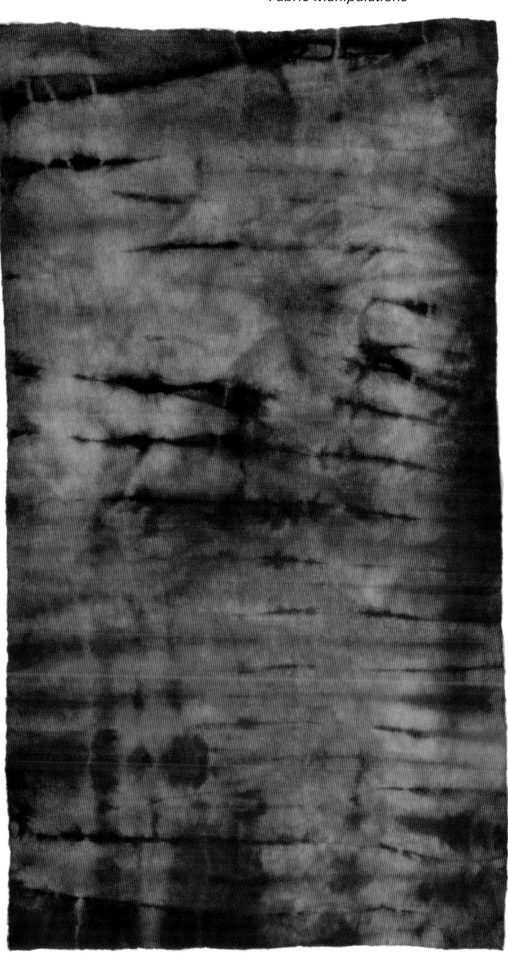

Shibori Folding Technique:
One-quarter yard of sunyellow
wool, using a fan roll. Colors
used: [119], [351], and [490] in
separate squirt bottles. These
bottles are kept on the stove
in a tray, with 1 tablespoon dye
added to hot water. Application
was randomly applied.

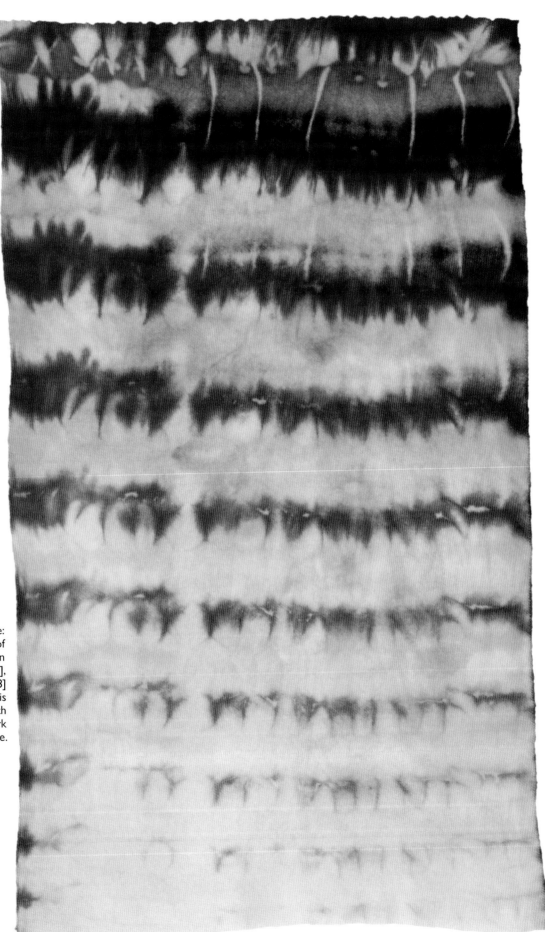

Shibori Folding Technique: One-quarter yard of natural wool, using a fan roll. Colors: [119, 1/16], [351, 1/32], and [490, 1/128] in separate beakers. This is like a Shibori dip dye, with the light, medium, and dark values in one piece.

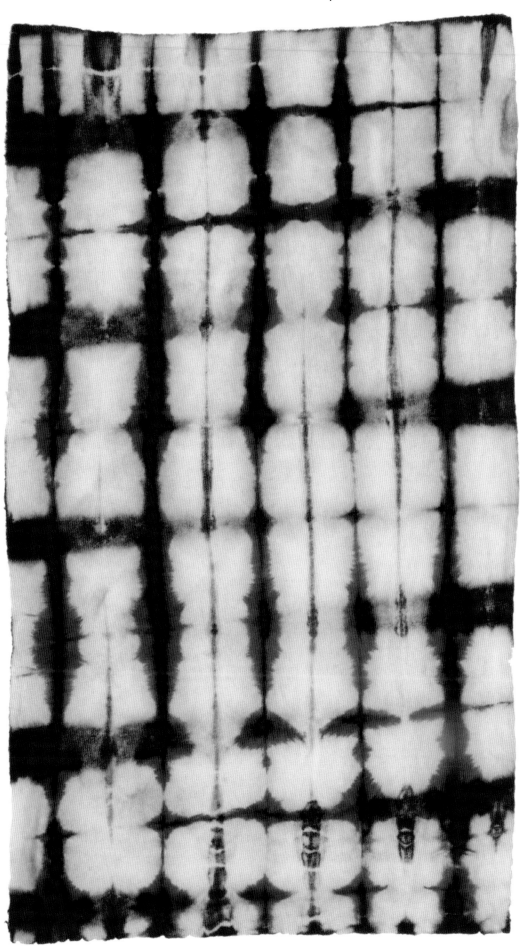

Shibori Folding Technique: One-quarter yard of natural wool, using colors [490] and [822]. By using a variety of ways to secure the folded Shibori wool, more or less definition will be provided. It is the experimentation that is so exciting.

Shibori Folding Technique: One-quarter yard of natural wool is on the left using a fan roll. Colors used: [817, 1/32] and [822, 1/32] in separate beakers. One-quarter yard celery wool is on the right, using triangle folds. Colors used: [119, 1/16], [199, 1/32], [440, 1/128], and, at the end, a squirt of yellow from the condiment bottle.

SHIBORI STITCHING TECHNIQUE

To make this book complete, I want to include this technique in the Shibori chapter. It is more time consuming than the folding, but less than the wrapping techniques. In this technique, needle and thread create the areas of resist to the dye on the wool. The stitches wander through the wool in any direction. As a quilter it is easy for me to use needle and thread to stitch and pull the wool so it wrinkles into a shape. I have done this style of stitching with a Baltimore Album quilt. The options for threading the wool are so varied.

I use an example from this year's class. Jackie Gauker, a quilt shop owner listed in the resources, was a student in my comprehensive dye class this year. We play after class time and her sewing skills resulted in a beautiful stitched Shibori. Jackie stitched the wool in a wave pattern.

I recommend using buttonhole thread or another thread with substance. Once the pattern is stitched onto the wool, one edge to another, leave a 4-inch tail of thread. This thread will be used to cinch the wool into a smaller size. Your stitching pattern may include many rows, or just a few. I have also used quilt safety pins to gather the wool as if it had been stitched.

This is simply another exciting way to play with color application, as you create areas of resist on the wool. The patterns that are possible from stitching different paths on the wool are unlimited. The stitching does not have to be perfect. Enjoy.

Fine examples hanging to dry. On the left a Shibori Stitching Dye Technique and right a Kettle Spot Dye Technique. More color parties to come.

Shibori Stitching Technique:
The randomness of the
thread and needle allow for
many explosions of color.
These wools may be cut in
the vertical or horizontal
direction depending on need.

Gather:

- wool, dry, quarter yard swatch
- 2-inch half hotel dye pan
- 2 beakers
- dry dye powder, 2 colors
- large eye needle
- buttonhole thread
- CA crystals
- Synthrapol
- Bluettes™ gloves

Start:

- Fill the dye pan one-third full of water, Synthrapol, and 1 tablespoon CA crystals.
- Simmer, without boiling, to dissolve the crystals.
- Make your colors in separate beakers; there is no limit.
- On a flat surface, stitch your wool as desired.
- When finished stitching, gently pull the threads from all directions and secure.
- The bubble side of the wool faces down, into the dye pan, allowing the water to be absorbed into the wool.
- Pour your first color into the dye pan. You may decide to pour the color directly on the wool, as the placement of color in the pan creates the magic in the end. If you plan to turn your wool over, and repeat the application on the other side, you might only use half of your dye bath on each side.

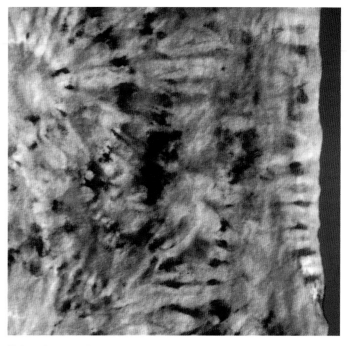

Shibori Stitching Technique: One-quarter yard natural wool, stitched in a wave pattern, leaving thread tails at the edge of the wool. The wool was cinched together and dyed in a shallow pan with 2 colors. Sewn and dyed by Jackie Gauker, owner of The Quilter's Palette, Fleetwood, Pennsylvania, by permission. *Courtesy of Jackie Gauker.*

- When ready, add the next color into the pan or directly on the wool.
- When the water is clear, add more water to bring the level to two-thirds of the height of the wool.
- Simmer, without boiling, for one hour and cool.
- Wash with detergent, rinse well, and dry.

1. Shibori Stitching Technique: dye pan with Synthrapol and 1 tablespoon CA crystals heating to temperature, dry wool stitched, and 2 or more colors. The stitching is random as shown with black thread.

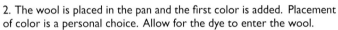

2. The wool is placed in the pan and the first color is added. Placement of color is a personal choice. Allow for the dye to enter the wool.

3. The second color is added randomly, then simmers, without boiling, one hour. Wash with detergent, rinse well and dry.

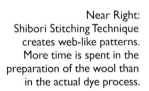

Near Right:
Shibori Stitching Technique creates web-like patterns. More time is spent in the preparation of the wool than in the actual dye process.

Far Right:
Shibori Stitching Technique: this wool and the wool in the previous picture were dyed in the same pan, yet the color traveled onto the wool differently. The thread acts as a resist to the dye in this technique.

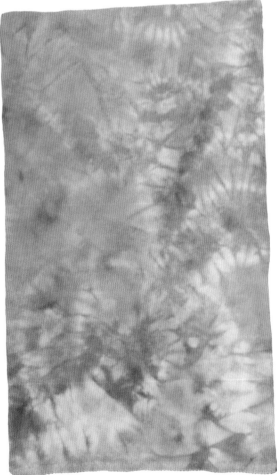

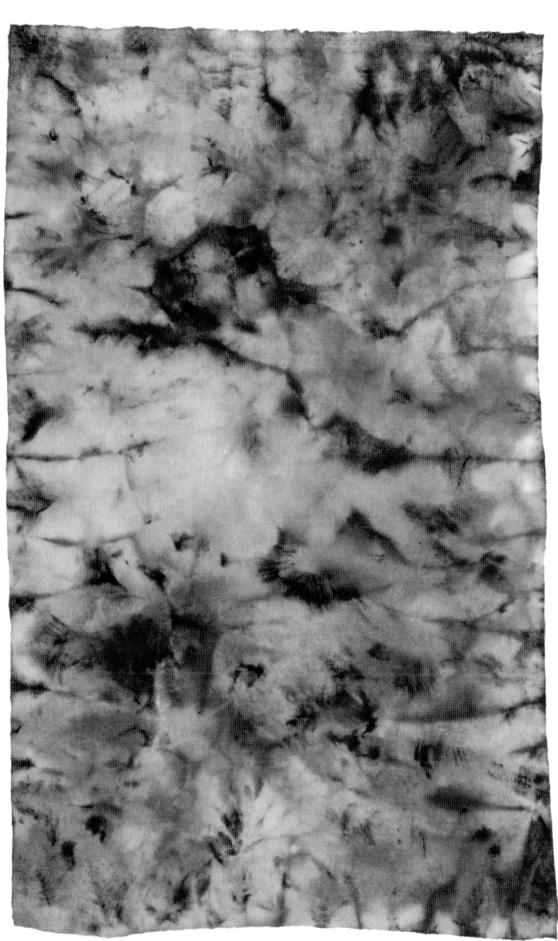

Shibori Stitching Technique:
over solid white wool, has
to be a favorite. It is fantastic
how the color is moving
through the wool to create
such interesting patterns.

Shibori Stitching Technique: A loose stitching of the wool swatch will result in fewer color patterns. A weaker dye bath, less dry dye, or more water reduces the intensity of the color in the finished wool.

SHIBORI WRAPPING TECHNIQUE

If you just completed the Shibori folding or stitching, you see what fun these techniques are. The wrapping takes a little more time to manipulate the wool, but it is worth the effort.

I sit in the evening and wrap the wool, then I dye it the next day. It is very calming to wrap glass cubes, rocks, or marbles; you may even warp around a finger. Thin floral wire cut into 6-8 inches pieces works best for me, but you might try other products. One student mentioned rubber bands; I have not tried this, but many different items work. Use your imagination.

Gather:

- wool, a dry, quarter yard swatch
- 2-inch half hotel dye pan
- 2 beakers
- dry dye powder, 2 colors
- floral wire, twine, or string
- small rocks, glass cubes, or circles; any variety is fine
- CA crystals
- Synthrapol
- Bluettes™ gloves

Shibori Wrapping Technique: Natural and tan wool. Wow. These turned out like a spring garden. You may want to use 2 colors for each wool swatch.

Shibori Wrapping Technique: One-quarter yard of celery wool, wrapped in rocks. Colors used: [490, 1/128] + [119, 1/8] and [119, 1/16] in separate beakers. Starting with pastel wool adds another color and value to the results.

Shibori Wrapping Technique: One-quarter yard of tan wool, wrapped with rocks. Colors used: [351, 1/8] + [402, 1/128], and [672, 1/64] in separate beakers. A scarf or wrap would be stunning with this technique.

Start:

- Cut floral wire 6 to 8 inches in length.

- Wrapping dry wool ahead of time is best. Place your item to be wrapped in the center of the wool, and secure it with the floral wire by wrapping the wire and creating a neck around the item.

- Continue this wrapping and securing until the entire piece of wool is wrapped. You may decide to wrap so that all of the wrapped bits are on one side of the wool; it will look like mushrooms on the surface.

- Fill the dye pan one-third full of water, Synthrapol, and 1 tablespoon CA crystals

- Simmer, without boiling, to dissolve the crystals.

- Make your colors in separate beakers, adding boiling water to dissolve the dry dye powder. I normally use 2 colors, but there is no limit to the number of colors.

- Lay your wrapped wool, mushroom side down, in the dye pan and adjust the water amount. I prefer not to have the water cover the top of the wool swatch.

- Add your first color into the pan or onto the wool.

- Allow the pan to clear of color.

- Add the next color with the same side down in the dye pan or turn the wool over and add the color. Protect your hands with gloves as you turn the wool.

- You may turn the wrapped wool over and add a third color.

- After the last color is added, simmer, without boiling, for one hour.

- Pour the wool into the sink and cool.

- With gloves on, unwrap the floral wire and remove the item that was wrapped. If there are large areas of undyed wool, or if starting with natural wool, you may decide to over-dye the entire wool swatch in a very light wash of another

Shibori Wrapping Technique using glass cubes and textured wool. The dark and light centers result from the wool going into the pan mushroom side down. *Wool donated by Pat Cross.*

color. If you add more dye, it would simmer, without boiling, one hour.

- Wash with detergent, rinse well, and dry.

1. Shibori Wrapping Technique: wrapped dry wool, dye pan with water, Synthrapol, and 1 tablespoon dissolved CA crystals, and 2 colors. The dry wool is wrapped around rocks, glass, or fingers. A variety of sizes and shapes are then tied off with floral wire, twine, or wool strips. Experiment with different items to find what works best for you.

2. This represents the "mushroom" look the wool will have when it is ready to dye in the Shibori Wrapping Technique. Add the first color into the pan and bring the water to a simmer without boiling.

3. Place the wool into the pan and allow the water to clear. By starting with textured wool the reward is a different tone or shade of the true color.

4. Add the second color directly on the wool to create interest and contrast when the wool is finished.

5. When the water in the dye pan is very weak, I like to remove the wire to expose the undyed area. Though shown here without gloves for clarity, the wool is very hot...use gloves!

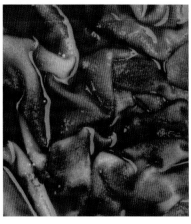

6. The wool is returned to the dye pan and simmers, without boiling, for one hour. If rocks or other solid items were used to wrap, allow the wool to cool prior to unwrapping. Wash with detergent, rinse well and dry.

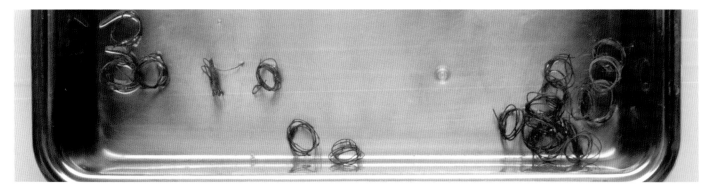

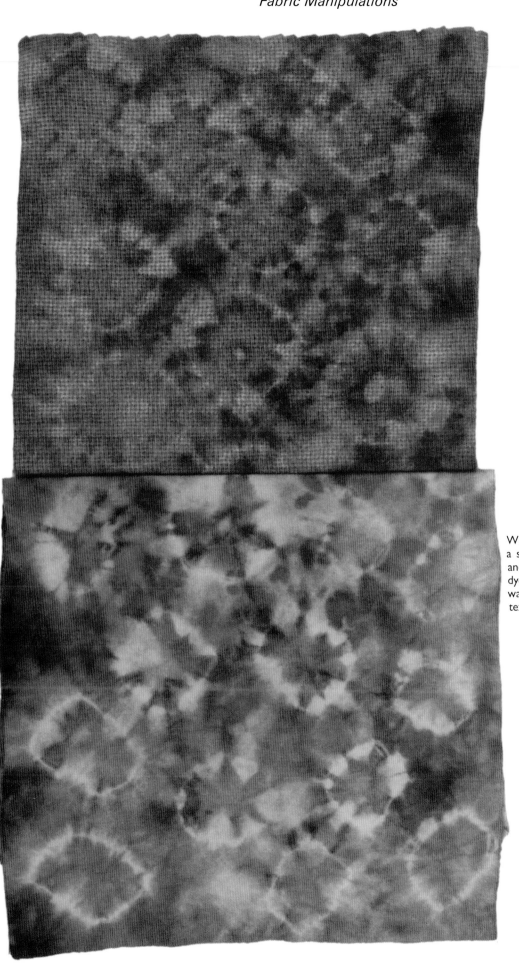

Wrapping Shibori Technique: a solid white on the bottom and textured wool on the top dyed together. The solid wool was finger wrapped and the textured wool used rocks.

Shibori Wrapping Technique: One-quarter yard of natural wool using large rocks. Colors: [502, 1/32] and [672, 1/64]. The size of the rocks also create added dimension. This inspiration came from former student and friend, Phyllis DeFelice. Phyllis gifted to me the large rocks. Amazing results!

Shibori Wrapping Technique: One-quarter yard of sunyellow wool, finger wrapped. Colors used: [233, 1/16] and [672, 1/128] in separate beakers. Pastel or light textures creating the lightest value.

Shibori Wrapping Technique:
It appears as if the light and
sun are bursting through the
wool. This is the front side
of the wool. You can see the
centers where the glass cube
was secured.

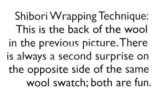

Shibori Wrapping Technique:
This is the back of the wool
in the previous picture. There
is always a second surprise on
the opposite side of the same
wool swatch; both are fun.

Shibori Wrapping Technique: One-quarter yard of celery wool wrapped on glass cubes. Colors used: [819, 1/32]. The actual item wrapped helps to create individual results. It is a purple paradise!

TWICE-COOKED COLOR

T his chapter is about the wool being braided together, with and without dye, pulling the color out of the wool into the dye pan, only to be sent back into the wool later. Very often, my dye pans contain a variety of textures, solids, and whatever may be near the dye pans. I have had many students with amazing resources find bits of wool waiting for something exciting to happen to it. This is one of those techniques.

This is just the technique all those red skirts found in recycled wool are waiting for. Enjoy this technique with a variety of combinations.

BRAID AND TWIST TECHNIQUE

If you have taken a class with Patsy Becker, you have witnessed this technique. Patsy is very dear to my heart and her zest for the dye pans amazed me. This technique uses any wool: textured, solids, and recycled. Most everyone has braided something in their lives and this is the same.

Some individuals are skilled with braiding 4 pieces of wool, so do not feel limited by three. This technique may be accomplished two ways. In the first, create a braid and add color to it like the overdye technique. The second way is to pull the existing color out into the pan with Tide and then send it back in with CA crystals.

Having covered the overdye process in the first technique, I will guide you through the braid with Tide. It will help to have at least one dark color or even red in the braid, as the color pulls out easier with darker wools. The braid may be twisted as you work towards tying off the second end.

Braid and Twist Technique: Dark green and purple wools were braided and then twisted prior to going into the dye pan. It is possible to braid more than three swatches.

Gather:

- wool, in quarter yards, dry
- 4-inch half hotel dye pan
- twine or string
- dry Tide laundry detergent
- CA crystals
- Synthrapol
- Bluettes™ gloves,

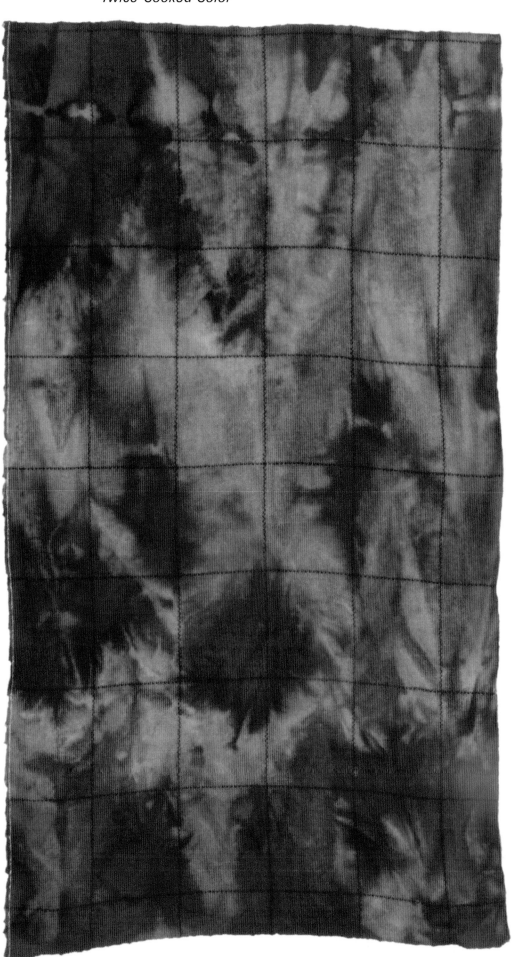

Braid and Twist Technique: One-quarter yard each of bright yellow, black, and red wool, twisted, and braided. This is my favorite combination. Some dark wool is necessary without dye.

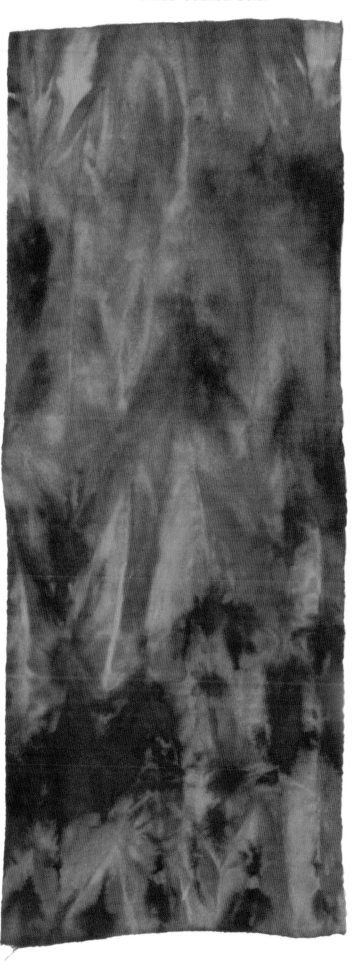

Braid and Twist Technique:
One-quarter yard of natural
wool twisted and braided
with purple and green wool.

Start:

- On a flat counter, have the empty dye pan close by with 1 teaspoon dry Tide and Synthrapol in the pan bottom.

- Gather several pieces of wool together and tie one end with twine. These may be twisted then braided or knotted together.

- Tie the other end together with twine.

- Place the wool into the dye pan and add water into the pan to half the height of the wool. Water will be absorbed into the wool, so before placing the dye pan on the stove, check the water level.

- If you did not use dark color wool that will leach out color, make a dye bath and pour it into the dye pan.

- Cover and simmer, without boiling, for 30 minutes.

- Uncover and, with gloves on, carefully turn the wool over.

- Dissolve 1 tablespoon CA crystals in hot water and add to the dye pan.

- Check the water level and bring the water height to be two-thirds the height of the wool.

- Simmer, without boiling, for one hour.

- Wash with detergent, rinse well, and dry.

1. Braid and Twist Technique: dye pan, water with Synthrapol and 1 teaspoon dry Tide detergent heating in it, dry wool braid with one dark color, twine, and CA crystals.

2. The braid is placed into the dye pan. Bring the water level to half the height of the wool as it becomes wet.

3. **4.** **5.**

3. Cover the wool and simmer, without boiling, for 30 minutes.

4. Dissolve CA crystals in a beaker of water. The Tide detergent pulls the color out of the dark wools. Add water without covering the wool.

5. With gloved hands, turn the wool over. Add CA crystals to the dye pan. The color returns to the wool very differently than it came out. Simmer one hour without boiling, cool, and then untie the surprise. Wash with detergent, rinse well, and dry.

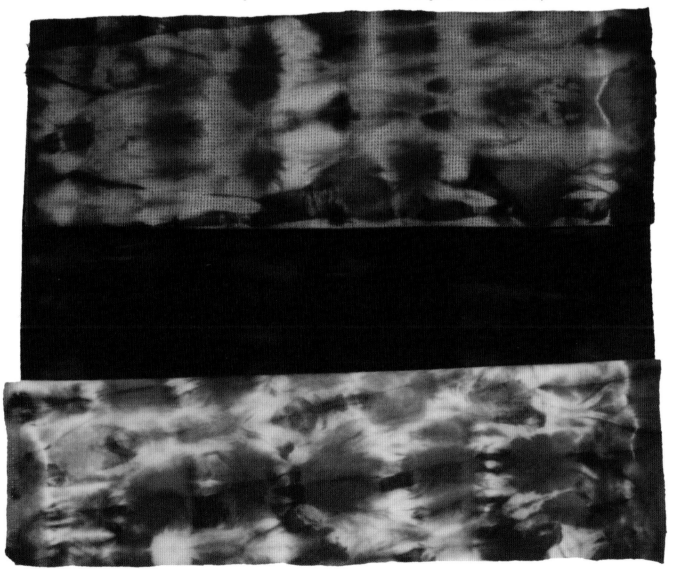

Braid and Twist Technique: The combinations of wool are what make this technique so exciting and very unexpected.

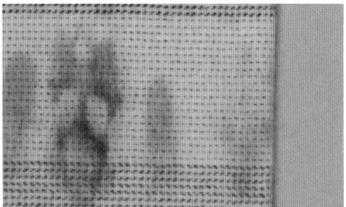

1. Braid and Twist Technique: dye pan with Synthrapol and dissolved CA crystals in the water heating, a variety of dry wool twisted and braided the ends tied with twine, 2 or more colors.

2. Place the first color into the pan and add the wool braid. Allow the water to clear.

3. The second color is added to the pan and the wool braid is turned over using gloves. The wool is very hot. Simmer one hour without boiling. Wash with detergent, rinse well, and dry.

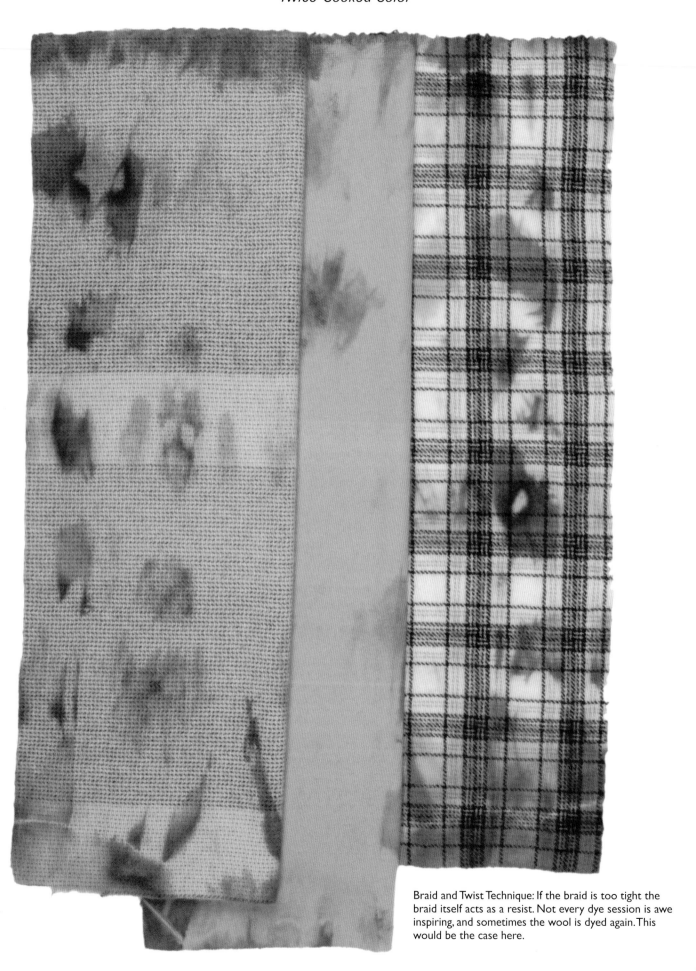

Braid and Twist Technique: If the braid is too tight the braid itself acts as a resist. Not every dye session is awe inspiring, and sometimes the wool is dyed again. This would be the case here.

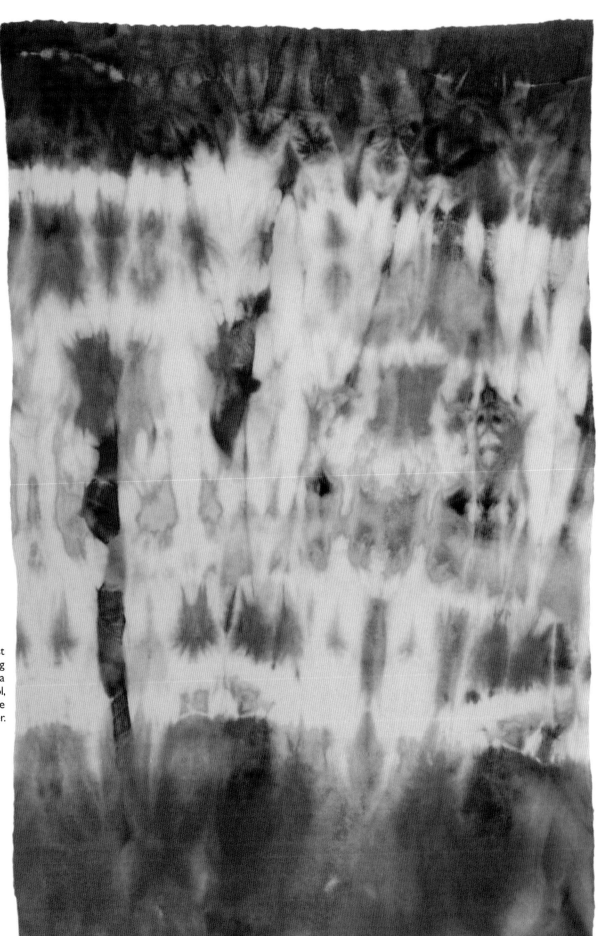

Braid and Twist
Technique: By starting
the technique with a
lightly colored wool,
the color contrast are
greater.

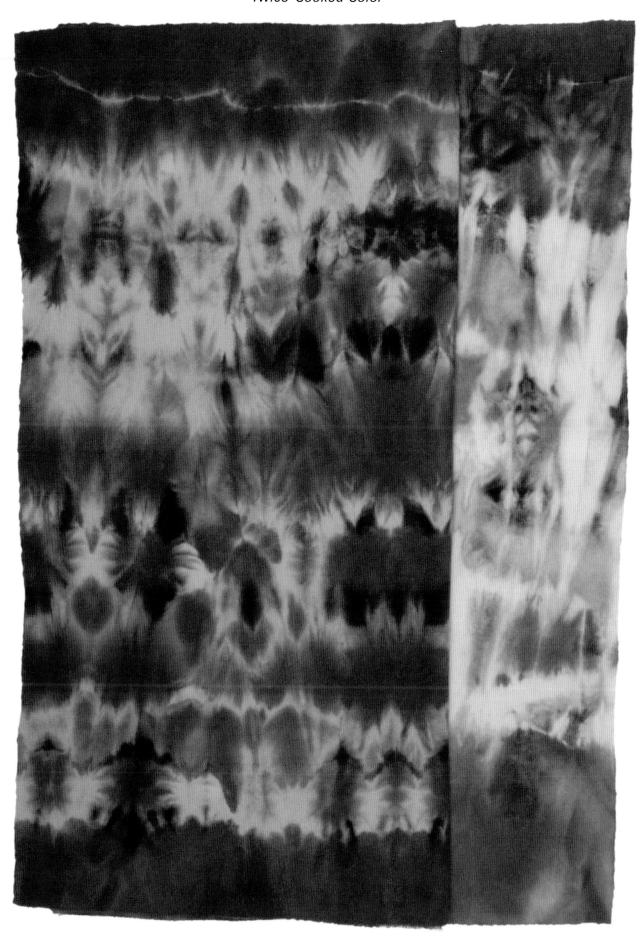

Braid and Twist Technique: Even Patsy Becker would be proud, she taught this technique to me. Yummy!

Braid and Twist Technique: One-quarter yard of yellow textured wool. The highlights remain visible throughout the dye process.

Braid and Twist Technique: One-quarter yard of natural wool braided with purple and black wool. Both sides of the wool offer a variety, in value and intensity.

STAINS: UNLIKE THE PINK T-SHIRTS IN THE WASH

I want to mention a little about stains. As I am driving off early in the morning to see clients, I often find myself with a cup of tea in hand. It is great for me that I wear a lot of black. Other times, it's a dash over to the cold water to try to remove the stain, because today it may be a light colored shirt or pants. I have experienced a blueberry protein drink exploding in my lap while I was in the car.

Tea and coffee stains are most welcome when trying to age cotton for dolls. Sometimes we just need a little extra color, for a very light swatch of wool and a stain will do the trick.

The large rug in our living room has a yellow center, stained with onion skins. A portion of the top border of the same rug, has red onion stained wool. The color is very mellow. I created the stains by stewing the skins in a large pot to draw out the color, then straining off the skins. I then used the liquid to stain the wool. It is a quite a challenge for me to retrieve enough skins from the market, so today I choose not to use onion skin dyeing. There are many resources for other types of dyeing. I find at this time in my life I enjoy the Pro® Wash Fast Acid dyes the best.

Yes, you have made it to the end. Your stash will bring a smile to your face. I have witnessed so much excitement. One gal jumped in the air and clicked her heels. She found her independence in the dye pans. Congratulations.

Clean up is easy with a little Clorox® and water, minding any sensitivities and using gloves. The ReDuRan® Special, is a product by Stoko®, and may be purchased from PRO Chemical & Dye Inc.® to remove dye stains from your hands.

A combination of Paisley, Dry Dye, Color Overlay, and Rocks and Wool Techniques. The warm and cool colors complement each other and represent balanced color harmony.

Amazing wools out of the dye pans onto the clothes line with beautiful flowers in the background. These are the fantastic colors from the, 2009 Dye Pots in the Green House class this year. Thanks ladies.

Who says we don't know how to play? The ladies in the comprehensive week class, 2009. Pictured left to right: Linda Beaulieu, Jackie Gauker, Glenn Cotton, Sue Getchell, Kathy Kinsely, Robin Garcia and Elaine Fitch. You may notice Linda's yarn balls in front and nylon's dyed successfully sitting on top of her head, by *permission*.

THERE IS NEVER ENOUGH DYED WOOL!

In this last chapter, I want to touch on noodles, ugly ducklings, and balancing your stash. We seem to have affinities toward certain colors and are devoid of other colors in our wool stash. In the dye class, my goal is to have everyone work their way around the color wheel by working through the primary colors, then the secondary colors.

I find it interesting, to observe the students' color choices in their dyed wool. There is a variety of wool around the room, both in value and color intensities; light, bright, dark, and dull. It is proof to me that every one has made different choices, as they find their individual color voice.

DYE YOUR NOODLES

Sometimes we think a color may work in our rugs, only to find it does not. We have already cut the wool into strips and stored them in a basket or a bag. These are called noodles, though some choose to call them worms. I do not even like to say the word "worms" much less see them, so "noodles" wins out here.

One weekend, I went through my two buckets of noodles from past projects and separated them into color piles. I put each color in a separate bag. When I was remodeling my studio, a friend recommended hanging the noodles. I secured an old tobacco rack to the wall and hung the bags on the hooks. It is now called, Noodle Row. Students swap noodles if they need a certain color, taking one out and putting one in.

Noodles can be overdyed, but it requires a gentle hand. Treat them like yarn: not much stirring, a little color at a time. I recommend the 2-inch half hotel dye pan. All the guidelines for proper setting apply: water, CA crystals, Synthrapol, color, time, and temperature.

I highly recommend that, when drying noodles, you consider how much they will be handled; less is better. Our dryer has a shelf that may be placed inside the dryer. The air is then circulated around the noodles that sit on a towel. Another option is to lay the noodles on a towel and place the towel outside in the shade to air dry. If you have made home made pasta, you know it hangs to dry; each pasta noodle is placed on the drying rack. You may also decide to hang each noodle on a clothes drying rack. The noodles may puff a little in your next project, but this is not necessarily a bad thing.

UGLY DUCKLINGS TURNED SWANS

Sometimes we just wonder what we were thinking when we bought that ugly wool. What do you do with the ugly ones? I recommend that students bring those wools to class. It is a fun challenge to turn the wools into something you love and that becomes beautiful.

When looking at wool that is considered ugly or unusable and trying to decide what color you may want to dye it, ask, "What color do you see the most of?" Based on that color, I would first try a color that is on the same side of the color wheel, an analogous color. My second choice is to overdye with yellow. My personal color palette is on the warm side of the color wheel, I usually default to a yellow or orange hue depending on the starting value of the ugly wool. Consider your favorites.

"Karen's Wool Garden," designed by Becky Trent, is my business logo. The sky is a color transition technique, hand torn, and hooked strip by strip. Thanks for visiting my wool garden, where colors grow wild.

Another way to deal with ugly wool is to put all the wools in one dye pan, add color, and simmer together. It is another way to experiment; if you do not like the color of a swatch, change it to one you like. I find the "unusable" wools turn out to be the greatest, once they are dyed.

BALANCED STASH

As individuals we have specific tastes in color. I love to see the varieties.

A balanced stash will contain warm and cool colors. In my studio, shelves hold the primary colors in a variety of hues, values, and intensities. Right next to the primary shelves are the shelves with secondary colors lined up beside their direct complement. The shelves act as a learning tool for the students to make color relationships as they hook. A picture of the wool in my studio is at the end of the chapter on color theory.

Color values and intensities are a personal choice. When signing up for a two-year quilt class in South Carolina, I wanted to use home spun fabric in my Baltimore Album quilt. The teacher, as talented as she was, preferred jewel-tone fabrics as the traditional fabric of choice. These are very complex quilts, and two of the ten students preferred not to have jewel tones. I did end up with a home spun background and it does make me happy. My hope is that students find colors that make their heart sing.

If you find your stash contains only in the medium values, consider colors you enjoy and dye light and dark values to add to the others. When trying to balance your colors, use your color wheel. The Pocket Color Wheel® will show you many values on one color. Keep your color wheel close by and as you experiment with mixing colors and have color days. Your stash will quickly balance.

I also try to keep neutrals on hand. We need the neutral hues to allow our eyes to rest. Work with browns, blacks, tans, and grays in different values as you balance your wools.

Remember that color is everywhere. In a very short time you will develop a discerning taste for color, value, and intensity. Trust your instincts when you dye your wool. It is your color voice and you have a right to it enjoy it in whatever fibers you use. As my mother used to say, "can't never could, won't never would, I will try and does." Thank you, for allowing me to guide you on this dye journey.

"The mediocre teacher tells.
The good teacher explains.
The superior teacher demonstrates.
The great teacher inspires."

William Arthur Ward

My goal as a teacher is to inspire, thank you, to all of my students, teachers and friends.

This is perfect example of everyone's color voice being different. The wool dyed by the students in the 2009 Green Mountain Rug School, Dye Pots in the Green House class, held in Randolph, Vermont. The blend of Zina's beautiful flowers and the colors dyed in the wools are mesmerizing.

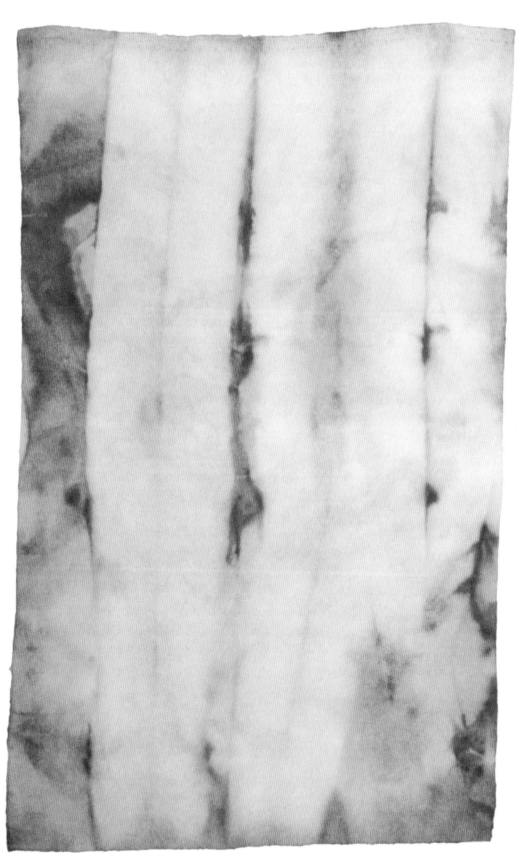

Shibori Folding Technique.

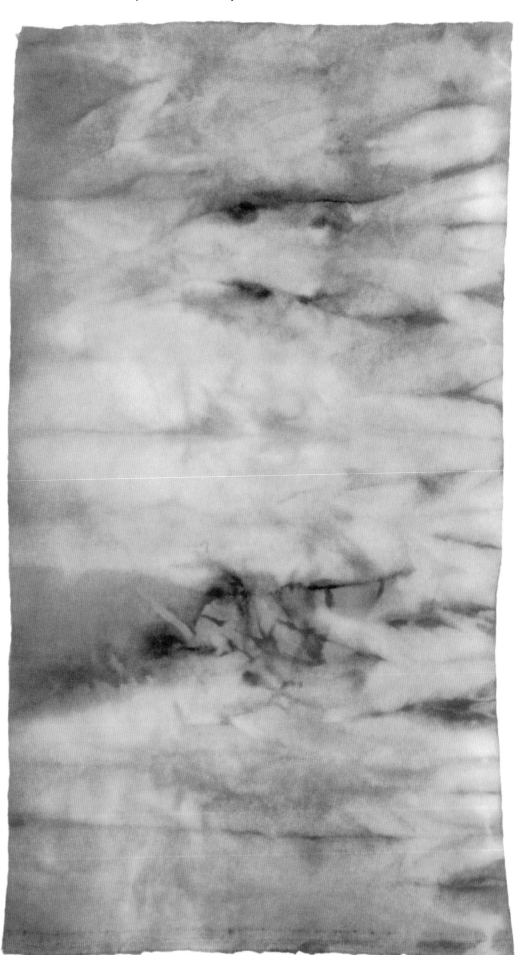

Shibori Stitching Technique

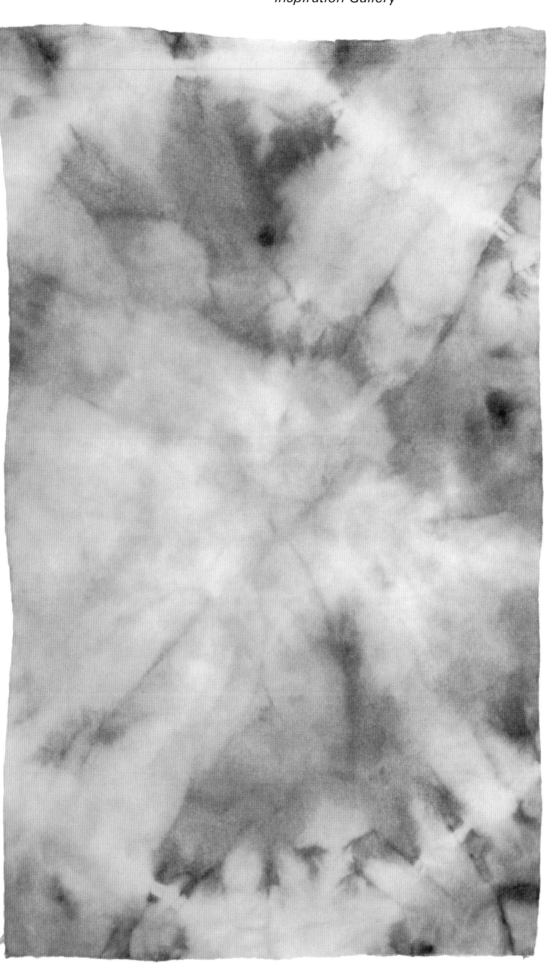

Shibori Stitching
Technique.

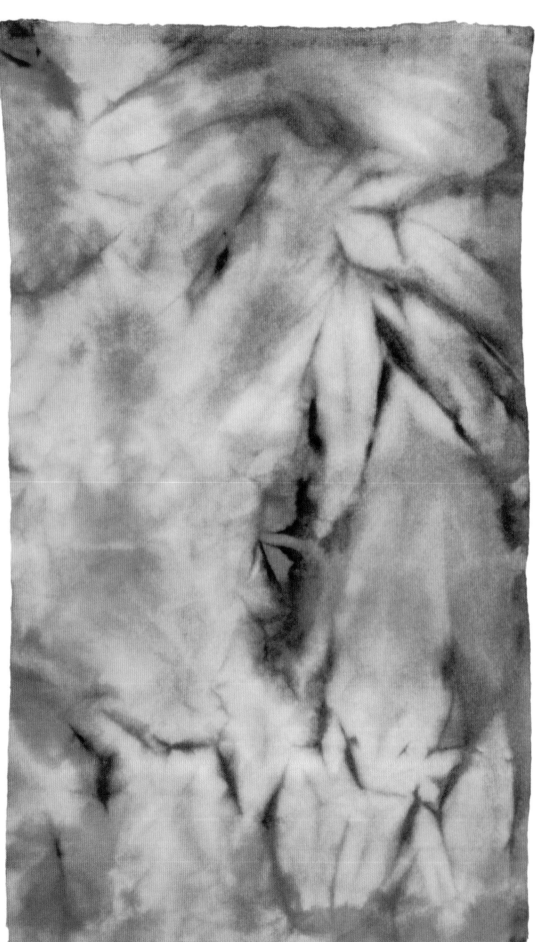

Shibori Stitching Technique.

Shibori Wrapping
Technique.

Shibori Wrapping
Technique.

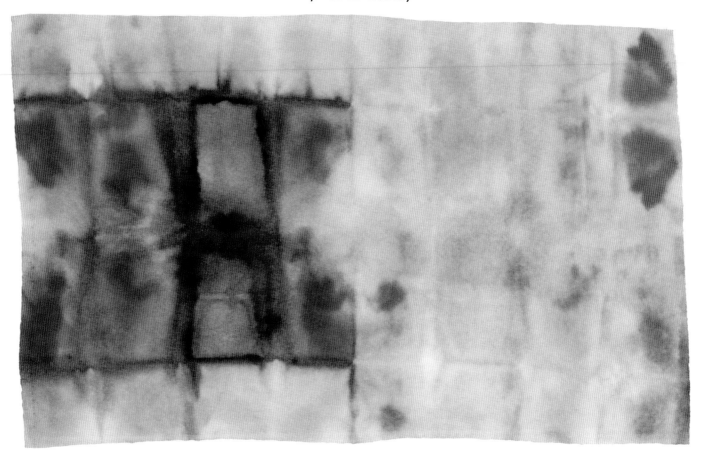

Shibori Folding Technique.

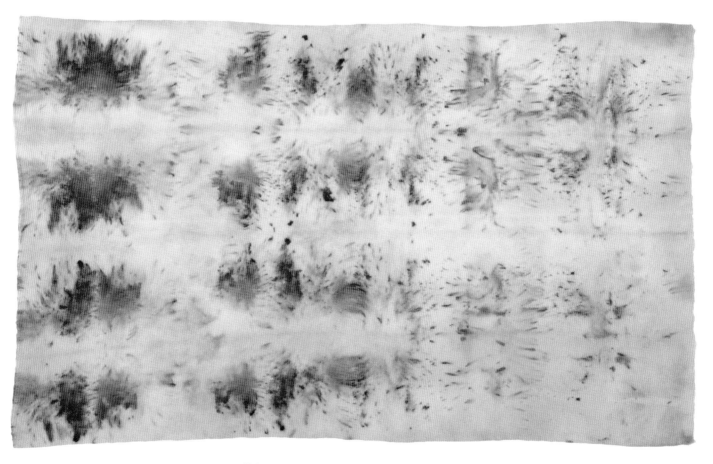

Shibori Folding and Floating Dry Dye Techniques.

Shibori Stitching and
Floating Dry Dye
Techniques.

Floating Dry Dye Technique

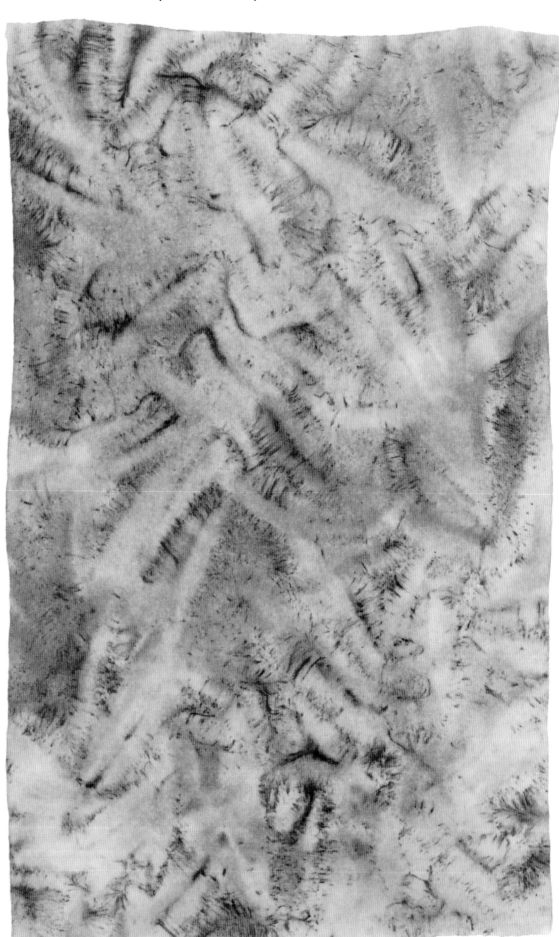

Shibori Stitching and Floating
Dry Dye Techniques.

Shibori Stitching and Floating
Dry Dye Techniques

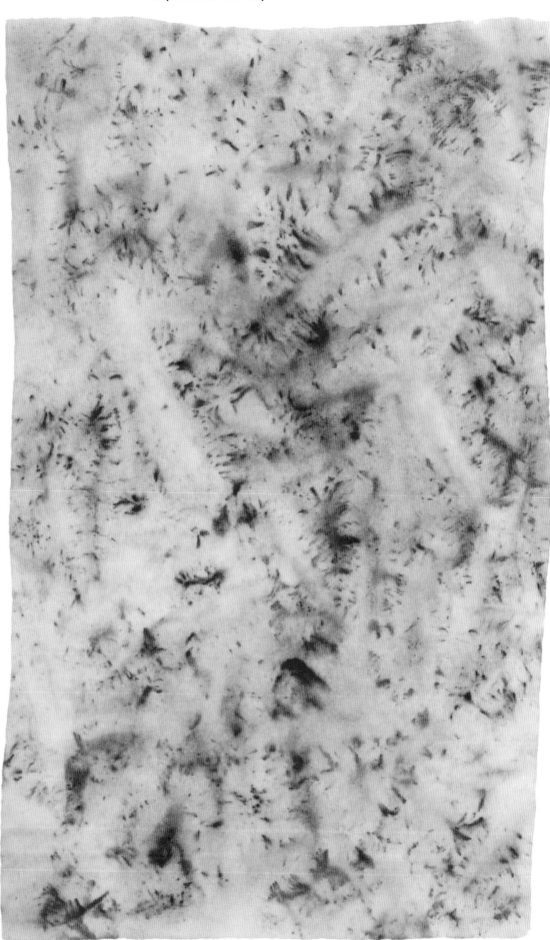

Floating Dry Dye Technique.

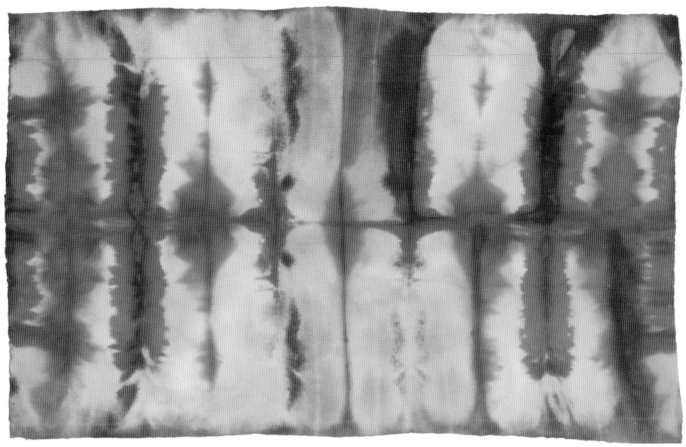

Shibori Folding Technique.

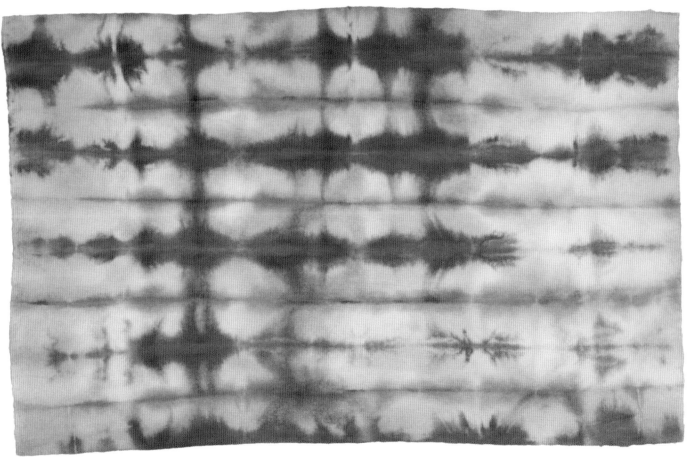

Shibori Folding Technique.

Shibori Stitching and
Floating Dry Dye
Techniques.

Floating Dry Dye Technique.

Floating Dry Dye Technique.

Shibori Wrapping Technique.

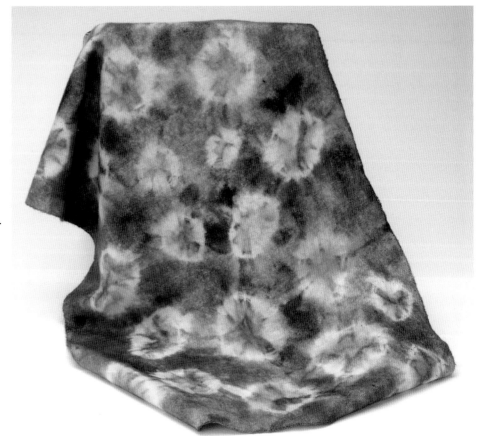

Shibori Stitching Technique.

Shibori Stitching Technique.

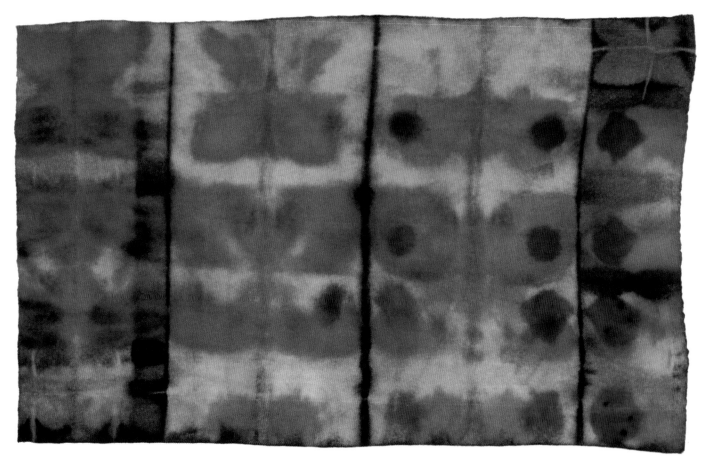

Shibori Folding Technique.

Shibori Stitching Technique.

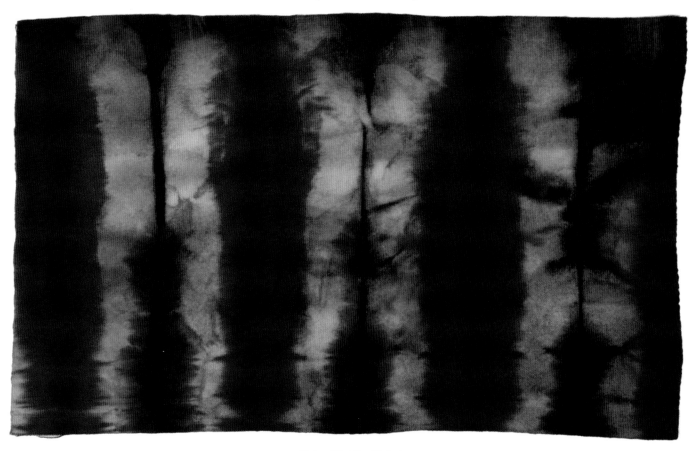

Shibori Folding Technique.

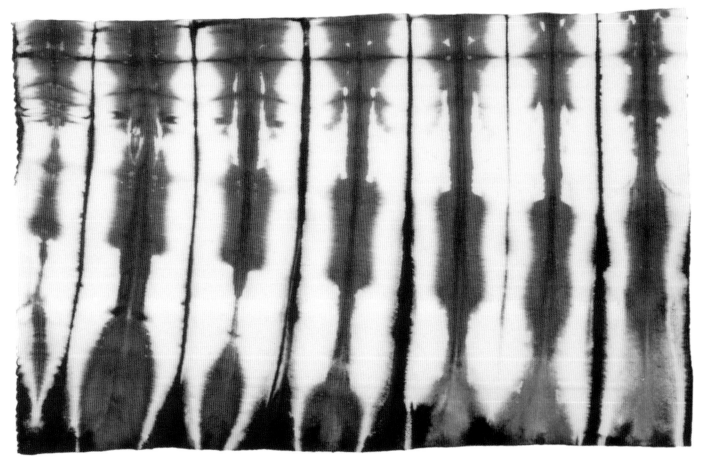

Shibori Folding Technique.

Shibori Stitching and
Floating Dry Dye Techniques.

Shibori Folding Technique.

Shibori Folding Technique.

Shibori Folding and
Floating Dry Dye Technique.

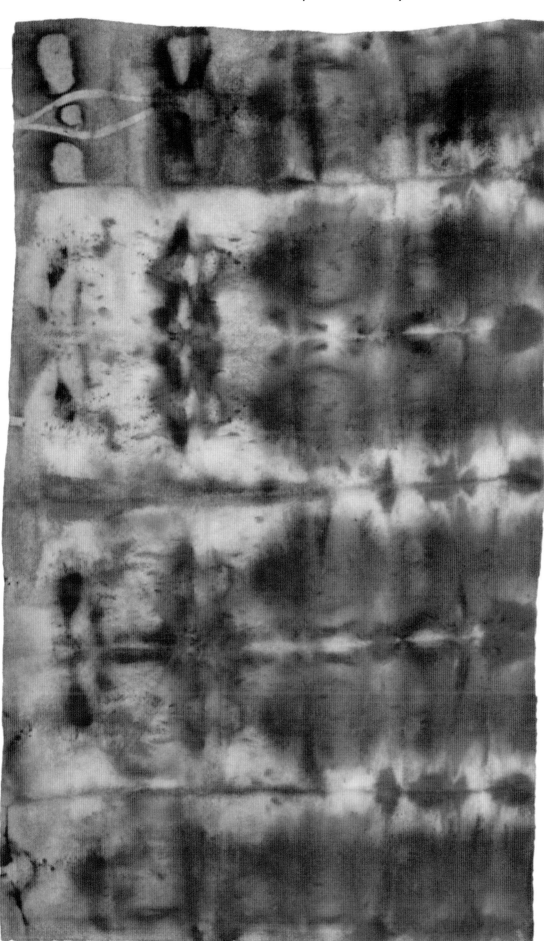

Shibori Folding Technique.

Shibori Stitching Technique.

Shibori Wrapping
Technique.

Shibori Wrapping Technique.

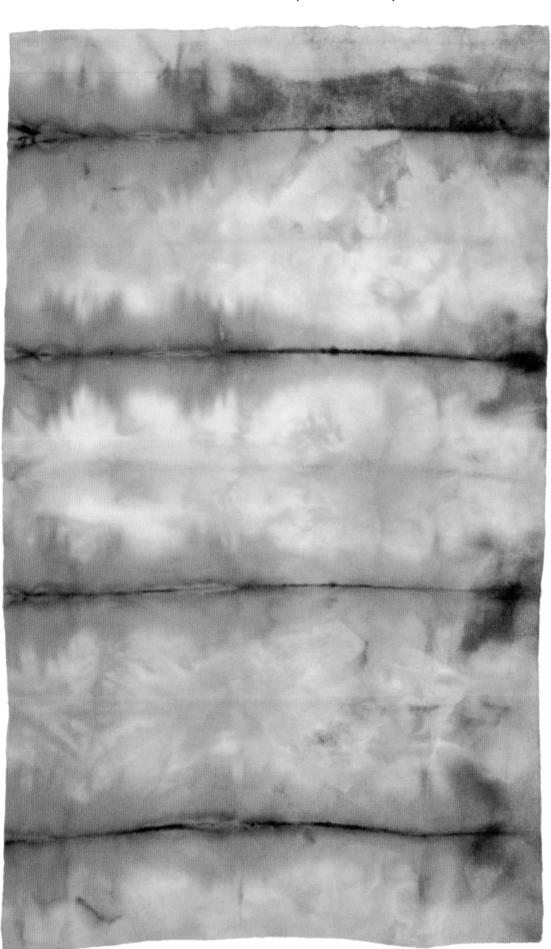

Shibori Folding Technique.

Shibori Stitching Technique.

Shibori Stitching
Technique.

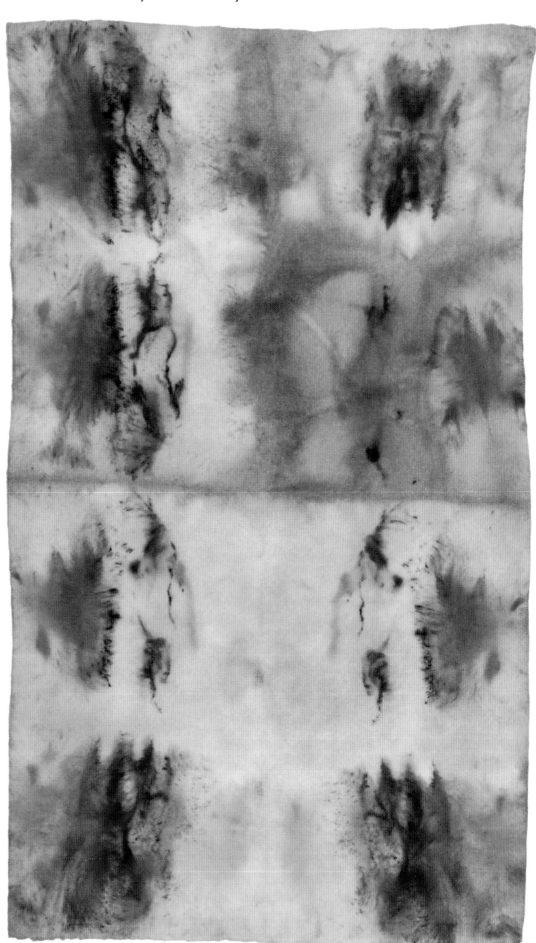

Shibori Folding and
Floating Dry Dye Techniques.

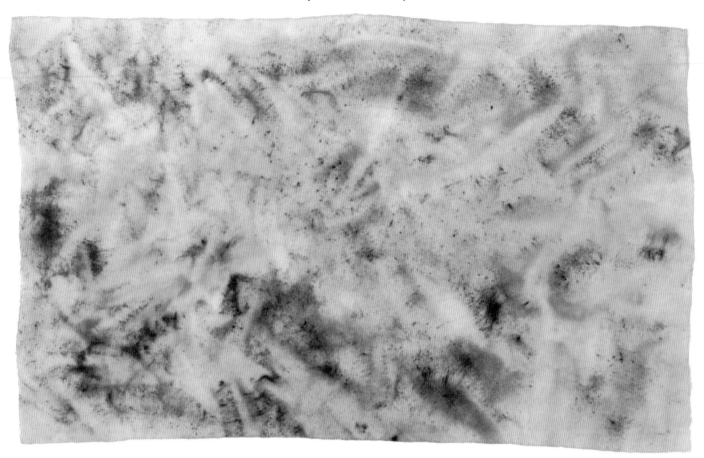

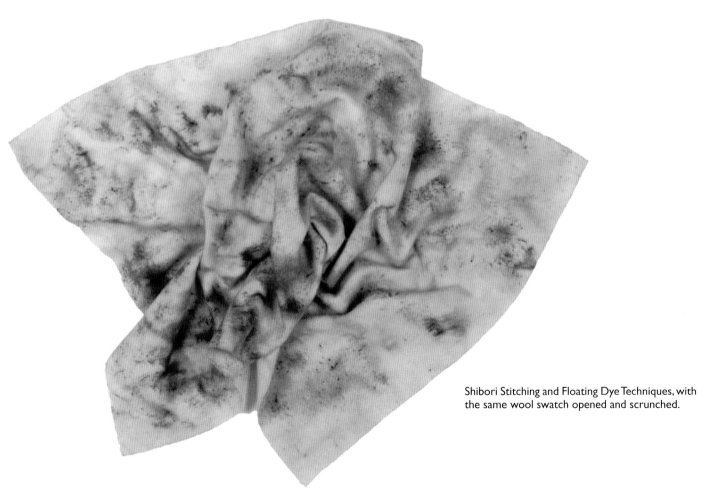

Shibori Stitching and Floating Dye Techniques, with the same wool swatch opened and scrunched.

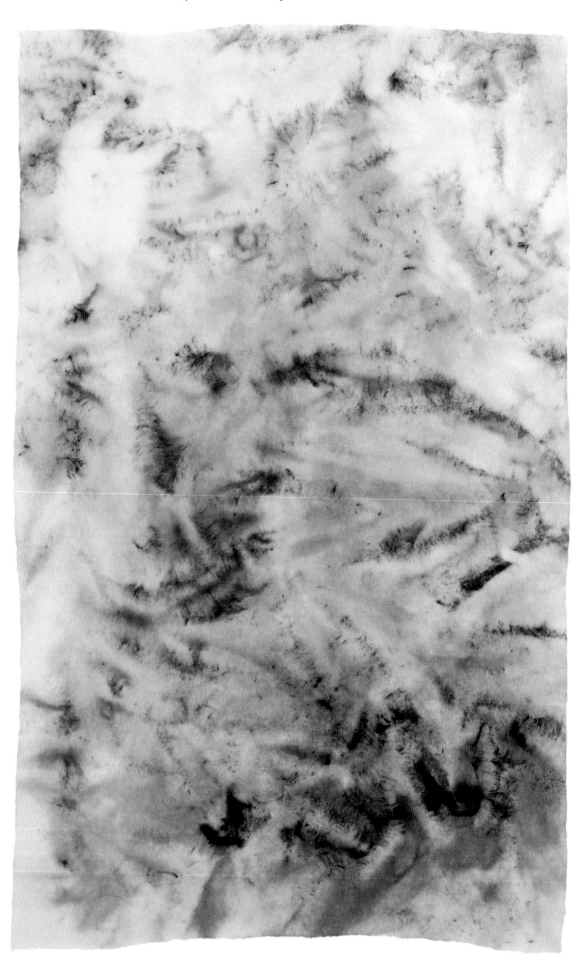

Shibori Stitching and
Floating Dry Dye
Techniques.

Floating Dry Dye Technique.

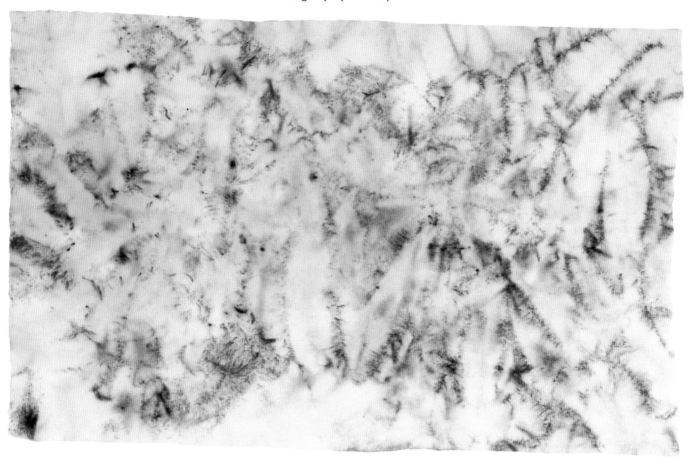

Shibori Stitching and Floating Dry Dye Techniques.

RESOURCES

Fluff & Peachy Bean Designs
Whimsical designs for rug hooking,
2126 US RT 7
PO Box 30
Pittsford, VT, 05763
802.483.2222
E-mail: ndjewett@verizon.net,
Nancy D Jewett, owner/designer

Green Mountain Rug School, Inc.
Rug hooking supplies, classes, accessories, & books
2838 County Road
Montpelier, VT, 05602
802.223.1333
Web: greenmountainhookedrugs.com
E-mail: vtpansy@greenmountainhookedrugs.com
Stephanie Ashworth Krauss, owner

Grey Dye Spoons
Polished aluminum dye spoons, 1/128 to 1 teaspoon
59 Wallace Street
Jackson, CA, 95642
209.223.7735
Douglas Grey, owner. A 30 year family business, started by Ralph and Gloria Grey. Ralph made the dye spoons by hand for 20 years.

The Quilters Palette
Quilt fabric, felted and dyed wool; quilt & penny rug
    patterns, books, and custom designs
3130 Pricetown Road, Suite L
Fleetwood, PA, 19522
610.929.3191,
Web: thequiltpalette.com
E-mail: thequiltpalette@aol.com
Jackie Gauker, owner

Harley Bonham Photography
Private, commercial, and corporate projects
602.254.1711
Web: harleybonham.com
E-mail: harley@harleybonham.com
Harley Bonham, photographer/musician

Karen's Wool Garden, LLC
Custom hand dyed wool, commissioned rugs, & classes
603 Wallace Ave.
Louisville, KY, 40207
502.435.4077
Web: karenswoolgarden.com
E-mail: karenswoolgarden@gmail.com
Karen Schellinger, colorist, fiber artist

Pennies from Heaven
Penny rug & rug hooking designs
612 Wallace Ave.
Louisville, KY 40207
502.523.2652
E-mail: christine.rabeneck@gmail.com
Christine Rabeneck, owner/designer

PRO Chemical & Dye®
Pro® WashFast Acid Dyes, auxiliaries, books
PO Box14
Somerset, MA, 02726
800.228.9393
Web: www.prochemical.com
E-mail: promail@prochemical.com

The Color Wheel Company™
Pocket Color Wheel™
PO Box 130
Philomath, OR
541.9297526
Fax: 541.929.7528,
Web: colorwheel.com
E-mail: info@colorwheel.com
Ken Haines, President

The Dorr Mill Store
Rug hooking & braiding supplies, accessories, books
PO Box 88
Guild, NH, 03754
800.846.DORR
Web: dorrmillstore.com
E-mail: contact@dorrmillstore.com
Terry Dorr, owner

Quail Hill Designs
Rug hooking supplies, designs, and classes
258 Pennellville Rd.
Brunswick, MA 04011
207.729.0299
Web: quailhilldesigns.com
Marion Ham, designer

Wool & Whimseys
Penny rug patterns, classes.
261 Center Hill Road
Plymouth, MA 02360
508.224.4961
Web:woodlandwhimseys@comcast.net
Karyn Lord, designer

SUGGESTED READINGS

Ames, Jim. *Color Theory Made Easy.* New York, New York: Watson, Guptil Publications, 1996

Barton, Jane, Mary Kellogg Rice, Yoshiko Iwamoto Wada. *Shibori.* Bunkyoku, Tokyo: Kodansha International Ltd., 1983

Carbonetti, Jeanne. *The Zen of Creative Painting.* New York, NY: Watson, Guptill Publications, 1998

Itten, Johannes., *The Color Star.* New York, New York: John Wiley & Sons, Inc, 1985

Powell, William F., *Color and How to Use It.* Laguna Hills, California: Walter Foster Publishing, Inc., 1984

Siegal, Connie Smith. *Spirit of Color,* New York, New York: Watson, Guptill Publications, 2008

Turbayne, Jessie A. *Hooked Rugs: History and the Continuing Tradition.* West Chester, Pennsylvania: Schiffer Publishing Ltd., 1991

Turbayne, Jessie A. *Hooked Rug Treasury.* Atglen, Pennsylvania: Schiffer Publishing, Ltd., 1997

Turbayne, Jessie A. *The Big Book of Hooked Rugs 1950 to 1980.* Atglen, Pennsylvania: Schiffer Publishing, Ltd., 2005

Turbayne, Jessie A. *The Complete Guide to Collecting Hooked Rugs: Unrolling the Secrets.* Atglen, Pennsylvania: Schiffer Publishing, Ltd., 2004

Turbayne, Jessie A. *The Hooker's Art.* Atglen, Pennsylvania: Schiffer Publishing, Ltd., 1993

Resting until the next dye class, see you then.
I hope you have been inspired,
Thanks for the visit.

—Karen Schellinger.

INDEX

From the dye pan to the clothesline, beautiful color and fresh air. Amazing women come to my classes, and my heart has been touched by all of you. Thank you.